COOKING *for* 1 OR 2

QUICK, EASY, DELICIOUS

Publications International, Ltd.

ISBN: 1-56173-776-3

Photography on pages 5, 17, 31, 45, 49, 52, 55, 61 and 71 by Janis Tracy Photography, Inc., Chicago, Illinois
Photographer: Janis Tracy
Food Stylist: Josephine Orba

Pictured on front cover: Chicken Scaparella (*page 44*).

Pictured on back cover (*clockwise from top right*): Chicken Rosemary (*page 51*); Miniature Cheesecakes (*page 88*); Fresh Strawberry Banana Omelet (*page 4*).

8 6 5 4 3 2 1

Manufactured in U.S.A.

Microwave ovens vary in wattage and power output; cooking times given with microwave directions in this publication may need to be adjusted. Consult manufacturer's instructions for suitable microwave-safe cooking dishes.

COOKING *for* 1 OR 2

QUICK, EASY, DELICIOUS

RISE 'N SHINE   4

LIGHTER FARE   16

MARVELOUS MEATS   30

PREMIER POULTRY   44

FROM THE SEA   60

PLEASING PLANNED OVERS   70

DAZZLING DESSERTS & DRINKS   82

ACKNOWLEDGMENTS   93

INDEX   94

RISE 'N SHINE

Greet the morning with this eye-opening collection of breakfast fare. Many can even be prepared in minutes for the late starter. Try "Fresh Strawberry Banana Omelets" tomorrow!

FRESH STRAWBERRY BANANA OMELETS

- **1 cup fresh strawberries, hulled and sliced**
- **1 banana, sliced**
- **1½ tablespoons sugar**
- **¼ teaspoon grated lemon peel**
- **1 tablespoon fresh lemon juice**
- **4 eggs**
- **¼ teaspoon salt**
- **¼ cup water**
- **2 tablespoons butter, divided**

Combine strawberries, banana, sugar, lemon peel and juice in medium bowl; mix lightly. Cover; let stand 15 minutes. Meanwhile, mix eggs, salt and water with fork in small bowl. Heat 1 tablespoon butter in 8-inch omelet pan or skillet over medium-high heat until just hot enough to sizzle a drop of water. Pour in half of egg mixture (about ½ cup). Mixture should set at edges at once. With back of pancake turner, carefully push cooked portions of edges toward center so that uncooked portions flow to bottom. Slide pan rapidly back and forth over heat to keep mixture in motion and sliding freely. While top is still moist and creamy looking, spoon ½ cup fruit mixture over half of omelet. With pancake turner, fold in half; turn onto heated platter. Keep warm. Repeat with remaining 1 tablespoon butter, egg mixture and ½ cup fruit mixture. Top omelets with remaining fruit mixture.

Makes 2 servings

Fresh Strawberry Banana Omelet

MEXICAN EGG MUFFIN

1 large egg
2 teaspoons water
1 teaspoon chopped green onion
1 teaspoon diet margarine
½ English muffin, toasted
1 slice BORDEN® Lite-line® Process Cheese Product, any flavor, cut into triangles
1 tablespoon prepared salsa

In small bowl, beat egg, water and green onion. In small skillet, melt margarine; add egg mixture. Cook and stir until egg is set. Spoon egg mixture onto muffin; top with process cheese product. Place on baking sheet; broil until process cheese product begins to melt. Top with salsa. Garnish as desired.

Makes 1 serving

Mexican Egg Muffin

CHEESE-BACON SOUFFLÉ

Grated Parmesan cheese
2 tablespoons butter
¼ cup chopped green onion
2 tablespoons flour
¼ teaspoon salt
⅛ teaspoon pepper
⅛ teaspoon garlic powder
1 cup milk
1 cup (4 ounces) shredded Cheddar cheese
3 egg yolks, slightly beaten
3 egg whites
¼ teaspoon cream of tartar
6 slices bacon, cooked, drained and crumbled

Preheat oven to 350°F. Butter a 1½-quart soufflé dish or casserole. Sprinkle enough Parmesan cheese in dish to coat bottom and sides evenly; remove any excess. Melt butter in medium-sized saucepan. Sauté green onion until tender, about 3 minutes. Blend in flour and seasonings. Remove from heat; stir in milk. Heat to boiling, stirring constantly. Boil and stir 1 minute. Remove from heat and stir in Cheddar cheese until melted. If necessary, return to low heat to finish melting cheese. (Do not boil.) Blend a little of hot mixture into egg yolks; return all to saucepan. Blend thoroughly; set aside. Beat egg whites until frothy. Add cream of tartar and beat until soft peaks form. Fold cheese sauce into egg whites. Fold in bacon. Turn into prepared soufflé dish. Bake 40 to 45 minutes. Serve immediately.

Makes 2 servings

Favorite recipe from **American Dairy Association**

ITALIAN OMELET

**1 can (8 ounces) DEL MONTE®
    Original Style Stewed
    Tomatoes**
1 teaspoon cornstarch
**½ teaspoon Italian herb
    seasoning**
4 eggs
**¼ cup water
    Salt and pepper, to taste**
**1 tablespoon butter or
    margarine**
**½ cup shredded Monterey Jack
    cheese**
**1 package (3 ounces) salami
    slices, slivered**
**1 can (4 ounces) sliced
    mushrooms, drained**
**2 tablespoons sliced green
    onion**
**2 tablespoons grated Parmesan
    cheese**

Combine tomatoes, cornstarch
and Italian herb seasoning. Cook,
stirring constantly, until thickened.
Combine eggs and water. Season
with salt and pepper. Heat butter in
skillet; add egg mixture and cook
slowly. Run spatula around edge,
lifting to allow uncooked portion to
flow underneath. When mixture is
set, sprinkle with Monterey Jack
cheese, salami, mushrooms and
green onion. Fold in half and turn
onto serving platter. Pour sauce
over omelet and sprinkle with
Parmesan cheese.

Makes 2 servings

Take-Along Breakfast Special

TAKE-ALONG
BREAKFAST SPECIAL

4 hard-cooked eggs, chopped
**¼ cup (1 ounce) shredded
    Cheddar cheese**
**2½ tablespoons bottled bacon-
    and-tomato flavored French
    dressing**
**2 to 4 toasted waffles, English
    muffin halves or bread
    slices**
Thin tomato wedges, optional
Parsley sprigs, optional

In small bowl, stir together eggs,
cheese and dressing. Cover and
chill to blend flavors. Spread half of
the egg mixture on each of 2
waffles. If desired, broil 6 inches
from heat in oven or toaster oven
until warm, about 3 minutes. Top
with additional waffles, if desired.
Garnish with tomato wedges and
parsley, if desired.

Makes 2 servings

Favorite recipe from **American Egg Board**

BREAKFAST PARFAIT

½ cup granola
¼ cup plain nonfat yogurt *or* cottage cheese
½ cup sliced strawberries
½ ripe banana, sliced

Place half of granola in parfait glass or glass bowl. Top with half of yogurt. Spoon half of strawberries over yogurt. Top with banana, remaining granola, yogurt and strawberries.

Makes 1 serving

Note: Recipe may be doubled.

PEANUT BUTTER-BANANA SHAKE

1 ripe banana, cut into chunks
2 tablespoons peanut butter
½ cup vanilla ice cream
1 cup milk

Place all ingredients in blender container. Cover; process until smooth.

Makes about 2 cups

BREAKFAST NOG

1¼ cups fruit pieces (fresh, thawed frozen or drained canned fruit can be used)
¾ cup milk
1 cup ice cubes
¼ cup NABISCO® 100% Bran
2 teaspoons sugar, optional

In blender container, combine fruit, milk, ice cubes, cereal and sugar, if desired. Blend at high speed 30 to 60 seconds or until ice is crushed and mixture is creamy. Serve immediately.

Makes 2 servings

EGGS JOSÉ

2 eggs
  Butter
2 tablespoons shredded Monterey Jack cheese
2 tablespoons bottled taco sauce
2 small *or* 1 large flour tortilla

In 7- to 8-inch omelet pan or skillet over medium-high heat, steam-baste eggs in butter. Top with cheese. Add small amount of water to pan; cover. Heat until cheese is melted. Spread sauce on tortilla. Top with eggs.

Makes 1 serving

Variations:
Eggs Giuseppe or Pizza Eggs: Substitute mozzarella or Parmesan cheese for the Monterey Jack cheese, pizza sauce for the taco sauce and toasted Italian bread slices or English muffin halves for the tortilla.

Eggs Joseph: Eliminate cheese and sauce. Substitute toasted bagel halves for the tortilla; spread with whipped cream cheese with smoked salmon or whipped cream cheese with chives. Top eggs with additional cream cheese, if desired.

Favorite recipe from **American Egg Board**

Breakfast Parfaits

MINI TURKEY HAM QUICHE

⅓ cup Turkey Ham, diced
¼ cup shredded reduced-calorie Cheddar cheese
1 (6-inch) frozen pie shell, prepared according to package directions
1 egg, beaten
¼ cup skim milk

1. Preheat oven to 350°F.

2. Sprinkle ham and cheese over pie shell. In a small bowl, combine egg and milk; pour evenly into pie shell.

3. On cookie sheet, bake quiche 20 to 25 minutes or until knife inserted in center comes out clean.

Makes 1 to 2 servings

Favorite recipe from **National Turkey Federation**

SAUSAGE BRUNCH CRÊPES

2 frozen Basic Crêpes (see page 72)
2 frozen sausage patties, regular or brown 'n serve
½ cup (2 ounces) shredded Swiss cheese
½ cup applesauce

remaining edges towards center, to form a square. Place, edge side down, in buttered baking dish. Sprinkle 2 tablespoons cheese over each. Bake 10 to 12 minutes or until cheese is melted. Meanwhile, heat applesauce in small saucepan until hot, stirring occasionally. To serve, spoon half of applesauce over each crêpe. Serve immediately.

Makes 2 servings

Favorite recipe from **American Dairy Association**

SAVORY EGG PUFFS

1 (8-ounce) carton EGG BEATERS® 99% Real Egg Product
2 teaspoons skim milk
3 teaspoons shredded reduced-fat Cheddar cheese
1 teaspoon chopped chives

Defrost egg product according to microwave defrost directions on carton. In each of 2 (6-ounce) lightly greased microwavable ramekins or custard cups, combine ½ container egg product and 1 teaspoon milk. Top each with 1½ teaspoons cheese and ½ teaspoon chives; cover. Microwave at HIGH (100% power) for 3½ to 4½ minutes or until puffed and set, rearranging twice during cooking. Serve immediately.

Makes 2 servings

MAKE-AHEAD FRENCH TOAST

12 eggs
½ cup milk
12 slices whole-grain or enriched
    bread
    Butter, optional
    Topping(s)

Beat together eggs and milk until well blended. Pour half of the egg mixture into 13×9×2-inch baking pan. Place 6 of the bread slices in the egg mixture. Turn slices and let stand until egg mixture is absorbed. Place on heavily buttered baking sheet. Repeat with remaining egg mixture and bread slices. Bake in preheated 500°F oven 6 minutes. Turn slices. Spread with butter, if desired. Continue baking until golden brown, about 3 to 4 minutes more. Serve immediately with preferred topping(s) or freeze* for later use.

Makes 12 French toast slices

Savory Topping Possibilities:
Thinly sliced beef, ham or
    luncheon meat
Canned meat spread, salmon, tuna
    or smoked fish
Thinly sliced cheese, cream
    cheese or cheese spread
Baked beans or chili
Sliced or chopped olives
Peanut butter

Sweet Topping Possibilities:
Sliced or chopped fruit
Applesauce
Chopped nuts
Toasted sesame or other seeds
Preserves, jam or jelly
Cinnamon sugar or confectioners'
    sugar
Coconut

*FREEZING INSTRUCTIONS: Cool toast slices on wire rack. Return to baking sheet(s). Freeze in single layer for 1 to 2 hours. Wrap in individual-serving portions or stack slices and wrap. Return to freezer. Store up to 1 month.

To serve frozen toast: Reheat single servings in toaster or place unwrapped slices on ungreased baking sheet(s) and bake in preheated 375°F oven until hot, 8 to 10 minutes.

Favorite recipe from **American Egg Board**

Make-Ahead French Toast

BAGEL TOPPERS

All of these versatile spreads and toppers can be made ahead of time and kept on hand for a quick breakfast anytime.

ORANGE-CREAM BAGEL SPREAD

- 1 package (8 ounces) cream cheese, softened
- 3 tablespoons orange marmalade

Combine cream cheese and marmalade in small bowl.

Makes about 1 cup

CHOCOLATE-CREAM BAGEL SPREAD

- 1 package (8 ounces) cream cheese, softened
- 3 ounces white chocolate, melted
- 2 tablespoons mini chocolate chips

Combine cream cheese and white chocolate in small bowl. Stir in chocolate chips.

Makes about 1¼ cups

CRAB BAGEL SPREAD

- 4 ounces cream cheese, softened
- 2 ounces crabmeat, shredded
- 4 teaspoons lemon juice
- 2 tablespoons chopped green onion tops
- 1 tablespoon milk

Combine all ingredients in medium bowl.

Makes about ¾ cup

PEANUT BUTTER TOPPER

- 2 tablespoons creamy peanut butter
- 1 tablespoon raisins
- 1 small banana, thinly sliced
- 1 tablespoon sunflower kernels

Spread bagel with peanut butter. Top with raisins, banana slices and sunflower kernels.

Makes 1 to 2 servings

HUEVOS CON SALSA

- 1 (8-ounce) carton EGG BEATERS® Cheez Omelette Mix
- 2 tablespoons ORTEGA® Diced Green Chiles
- 2 teaspoons FLEISCHMANN'S® Margarine
- ½ cup ORTEGA® Mild Thick and Chunky Salsa, warmed

In bowl, mix omelette mix and chiles. Prepare omelette according to label directions using margarine. Fill with half the salsa; fold and slide onto serving plate. Serve topped with remaining salsa.

Makes 2 servings

Top to bottom: Peanut Butter Topper; Crab Bagel Spread

HAM AND CHEESE QUESADILLAS

½ cup (2 ounces) shredded Monterey Jack cheese
½ cup (2 ounces) shredded Cheddar cheese
4 (10-inch) flour tortillas
4 ounces ham, finely chopped
¼ cup chopped canned green chilies
Salsa (optional)

1. Combine cheeses; divide equally between 2 tortillas. Place ham and green chilies over cheese. Top each with another tortilla.

2. Heat large skillet over medium heat. Add 1 quesadilla; cook until cheese starts to melt and bottom is browned, about 2 minutes. Turn over and cook other side until browned. Remove and keep warm while cooking remaining quesadilla. Cut each quesadilla into 8 wedges. Serve with salsa, if desired.

Makes 2 servings

PITA IN THE MORNING

1 teaspoon butter or margarine
2 eggs, lightly beaten
¼ teaspoon salt
Dash of pepper
1 whole-wheat pita bread, cut in half
¼ cup alfalfa sprouts
2 tablespoons shredded Cheddar cheese
2 tablespoons chopped tomato
Avocado slices (optional)

1. Melt butter at HIGH (100%) 30 seconds in microwave-safe 1-quart casserole.

2. Season eggs with salt and pepper. Add eggs to casserole. Microwave at HIGH 1½ to 2½ minutes, stirring once. Do not overcook; eggs should be soft with no liquid remaining.

3. Open pita halves to make pockets. Arrange sprouts in pockets. Divide cheese and eggs evenly between pockets. Top with tomato and avocado slices.

Makes 1 sandwich

CREAM OF WHEAT® À LA MODE

1 (1¼-ounce) packet Mix 'n Eat CREAM OF WHEAT® Cereal—Brown Sugar & Cinnamon
½ cup boiling water
½ cup mixed fresh fruit pieces
¼ cup vanilla yogurt

Prepare cereal according to package directions using boiling water. Top prepared cereal with fruit and yogurt. Serve immediately.

Makes 1 serving

EASY, ELEGANT EGG BAKE

  4 frozen patty shells
  4 eggs
¼ cup (2 ounces) dairy sour
    cream
  1 can (2 ounces) sliced
    mushrooms, drained
¼ teaspoon dill weed
    Dash of salt
    Dill sprigs for garnish

Begin to bake patty shells according to package directions. After 20 minutes, remove from oven. *Reduce temperature to 375°F.* Carefully remove centers of tops and soft dough underneath. Set aside.* Break and slip an egg into each shell. Continue baking until egg whites are almost set, about 14 to 15 minutes. Meanwhile, blend together sour cream, mushrooms and seasonings. Remove shells from oven. Spoon 2 tablespoons of the sour cream mixture over each egg. Continue baking until hot, about 3 minutes. Garnish with dill sprigs, if desired.

Makes 2 servings

*Bake tops alongside filled shells and serve as lids or accompaniments, if desired.

Favorite recipe from **American Egg Board**

CHOCOLATE CHUNK BANANA BREAD

  2 eggs, lightly beaten
  1 cup mashed ripe bananas
    (about 3 medium bananas)
⅓ cup vegetable oil
¼ cup milk
  2 cups all-purpose flour
  1 cup sugar
  2 teaspoons CALUMET® Baking
    Powder
¼ teaspoon salt
  1 package (4 ounces) BAKER'S®
    GERMAN'S® Sweet
    Chocolate, coarsely
    chopped
½ cup chopped nuts

HEAT oven to 350°F.

STIR eggs, bananas, oil and milk until well blended. Add flour, sugar, baking powder and salt; stir until just moistened. Stir in chocolate and nuts. Pour into greased 9×5-inch loaf pan.

BAKE for 55 minutes or until toothpick inserted into center comes out clean. Cool in pan 10 minutes. Remove from pan to cool on wire rack.

Makes 1 loaf

Prep time: 20 minutes
Baking time: 55 minutes

FREEZING INSTRUCTIONS: Slice bread and wrap in individual servings in freezer-weight wrap. Freeze for up to three months.

*L*IGHTER FARE

In search of a satisfying lighter meal? Try any one of these in-a-minute recipes for your next brown-bag lunch, light Sunday supper or last-minute snack.

TURKEY-CRANBERRY CLUB SANDWICHES

- **1 can (8 ounces) pineapple tidbits, drained**
- **1 can (5 ounces) chunk white turkey in water, drained**
- **⅓ cup grated carrot**
- **¼ cup chopped green pepper**
- **¼ cup chopped canned walnuts *or* almonds**
- **1 tablespoon chopped green onion**
- **3 tablespoons reduced-calorie mayonnaise**
- **¼ cup reduced-fat cream cheese, softened**
- **1 can (16 ounces) brown bread, cut into 12 slices (scant ½-inch slices)**
- **¼ cup canned whole berry cranberry sauce**

Combine pineapple, turkey, carrot, green pepper, walnuts and onion in small bowl; stir in mayonnaise.

Spread cream cheese on 4 bread slices; top with cranberry sauce. Add 4 bread slices; top with turkey mixture and remaining bread slices.

*Makes 2 servings
(2 sandwiches each)*

Variation: 1 can (6½ ounces) light tuna in spring water, drained, or 1 can (5 ounces) chunk white chicken in water, drained, can be substituted for the turkey.

Favorite recipe from **Canned Food Information Council**

Turkey-Cranberry Club Sandwiches

Garden Shrimp Salad

GARDEN SHRIMP SALAD

1½ cups broccoli florets
½ cup diagonally cut carrot
    slices
3 tablespoons water
½ cup snow peas, trimmed
3 tablespoons soy sauce
2 tablespoons lemon juice
2 to 3 teaspoons sesame oil
2 teaspoons sugar
1 teaspoon grated fresh ginger
1 cup medium pasta shells,
    cooked and drained
½ pound cooked, peeled and
    deveined medium shrimp
½ cup thin red pepper slices
2 green onions, chopped
2 teaspoons sesame seeds,
    toasted

Place broccoli and carrots in
1-quart microwave-safe casserole.
Add water; cover. Microwave on
HIGH 2 minutes; stir. Add snow
peas; cover. Microwave on HIGH
1 minute; drain. Cover vegetables
with ice water to stop further
cooking. Let stand 5 minutes;
drain. Combine soy sauce, lemon
juice, sesame oil, sugar and ginger
in large bowl. Add cooked
vegetables, pasta, shrimp and
peppers; toss lightly. Cover; chill,
stirring occasionally. Sprinkle with
green onions and sesame seeds
just before serving.

Makes 2 servings

GOLDEN HAM SANDWICH

4 slices buttered toast
4 slices cooked ham
½ cup mayonnaise
½ cup chopped celery
1 teaspoon chopped parsley
½ teaspoon curry powder
¼ teaspoon salt
2 Crispin apples
½ cup shredded Cheddar cheese

Place toast slices on cookie sheet
or on bottom of ovenproof dish;
top with ham slices. Combine
mayonnaise, celery, parsley and
seasonings. Spread over ham.
Wash, core and pare apples; cut
into very thin slices. Arrange apple
slices on top of mayonnaise
mixture; sprinkle with the cheese.
Broil just until cheese melts.
Serve hot.

*Makes 2 luncheon-size
open-faced sandwiches*

Favorite recipe from **Western New York
Apple Growers Association, Inc.**

SOFT TACO SANDWICHES

    4 (6-inch) flour tortillas
 ½ cup canned refried beans
    1 can (5 ounces) chunk white
       chicken in water, drained
 ½ cup (2 ounces) shredded
       Cheddar *or* Monterey Jack
       cheese
 ¼ cup chopped tomato
 ¼ cup canned chopped mild or
       hot chiles
    2 tablespoons sliced green
       onions and tops
 ½ cup thinly sliced iceberg
       lettuce *or* 4 large lettuce
       leaves

Spread each tortilla with refried beans. In a small bowl, combine chicken, cheese, tomato, chiles and green onions; spoon over refried beans. Top with lettuce and roll up.

*Makes 2 servings
(2 sandwiches each)*

Variation: 1 can (4¼ ounces) small shrimp or 1 can (6½ ounces) light tuna in spring water can be substituted for the chicken.

Note: For a hot taco sandwich, microwave sandwich on HIGH 1 minute or until cheese is melted.

Favorite recipe from **Canned Food Information Council**

JAPANESE BEEF SALAD

    2 beef tenderloin steaks, cut
       1 inch thick (about 4 ounces
       each)
    2 teaspoons oil, divided
    1 tablespoon teriyaki sauce
 12 fresh pea pods, blanched
 ¼ cup *each*: shredded cucumber,
       Japanese white radish
       (*daikon*)*
    1 teaspoon rice vinegar
       Thin sliced pickled red ginger
       (*benishoga*),* if desired

Heat heavy nonstick frying pan over medium heat 5 minutes. Add 1 teaspoon oil; swirl to coat bottom of pan. Add steaks and cook 4 to 5 minutes on each side. Brush teriyaki sauce over cooked sides of meat. Meanwhile, arrange pea pods, cucumber and radish in sectioned tray or on platter. Combine vinegar and remaining 1 teaspoon oil; drizzle over vegetables. Carve steak into thin slices and arrange in tray. Garnish with pickled ginger.

Makes 2 servings

Prep time: 15 minutes
Cook time: 8 to 10 minutes

*Available at Oriental markets.

Favorite recipe from **National Live Stock and Meat Board**

Japanese Beef Salad

South-of-the-Border Shrimp Salad

SOUTH-OF-THE-BORDER SHRIMP SALAD

1 avocado, halved
Crisp salad greens
½ pound cooked bay shrimp
1 DOLE® Orange, peeled, sliced
1 DOLE® Banana, peeled, sliced
1 cup cherry tomatoes

DRESSING
1 DOLE® Orange
1 lime *or* ½ lemon, juiced
2 tablespoons vegetable oil
1 tablespoon chopped cilantro
    or parsley
1 tablespoon chopped fresh
    mild green chile or canned
    diced green chiles
2 teaspoons sugar
¼ teaspoon paprika
¼ teaspoon chili powder
⅛ teaspoon salt

On 2 plates, arrange avocado halves on salad greens. Fill avocado halves with shrimp. Arrange orange, banana and tomatoes around avocado. Serve with dressing.

Makes 2 servings

DRESSING: Grate peel from ½ orange; juice orange to make ⅓ cup. In jar with lid, combine all ingredients. Shake until well blended.

VEGETABLE COTTAGE CHEESE SALAD

1 package (4-serving size)
    JELL-O® Brand Lemon
    Flavor Sugar Free Gelatin
1 cup boiling water
¾ cup cold water
1 tablespoon vinegar
1 cup (8 ounces) 2% lowfat
    cottage cheese
¼ cup chopped celery
¼ cup chopped green pepper
¼ cup chopped red pepper
¼ cup chopped carrot
¼ teaspoon onion powder
⅛ teaspoon black pepper

Completely dissolve gelatin in boiling water. Add cold water and vinegar. Measure 1 cup gelatin mixture; divide evenly among 2 individual plastic containers or serving dishes. Chill until set, but not firm. Add remaining ingredients to remaining gelatin. Chill until slightly thickened. Spoon over clear gelatin. Chill until firm, about 2 hours.

Makes about 3¾ cups or
2 entrée servings

GARDEN TUNA GRAZER

1 cup shredded carrots
1 can (6½ ounces) tuna, drained
    and flaked
½ cup diced zucchini
⅓ cup chopped walnuts
½ cup WISH-BONE® Creamy
    Italian Dressing
2 pita breads, halved
1 medium tomato, sliced

In medium bowl, thoroughly combine carrots, tuna, zucchini, walnuts and creamy Italian dressing; cover and chill. To serve, line breads with tomato, then fill with tuna mixture.

Makes 2 servings

Variation: For a *Garden Grazer*, substitute ½ cup creamed cottage cheese for tuna and decrease dressing to ⅓ cup.

THE CALIFORNIA CLASSIC

¼ cup KRAFT® Real Mayonnaise
1 teaspoon KRAFT® Pure Prepared Mustard
4 slices rye bread Alfalfa sprouts
4 LOUIS RICH® Oven Roasted Turkey Breast Slices
¼ pound VELVEETA® Pasteurized Process Cheese Spread, sliced Thin tomato slices Thin peeled avocado slices

• Mix mayonnaise and mustard.

• Spread bread slices with mayonnaise mixture.

• For each sandwich, top one bread slice with sprouts, turkey, VELVEETA® Pasteurized Process Cheese Spread, tomatoes, avocados and second bread slice.

Makes 2 servings

Prep time: 10 minutes

Variation: Substitute OSCAR MAYER® Salami Slices or Boiled Ham Slices for turkey.

The California Classic

CHEF'S SALAD

To julienne turkey and cheese, cut into matchstick-size pieces.

1 package (4-serving size) JELL-O® Brand Lemon Flavor Sugar Free Gelatin
¼ teaspoon salt
¾ cup boiling water
½ cup cold water
   Ice cubes
1 tablespoon vinegar
2 tablespoons reduced-calorie French dressing
¼ teaspoon Worcestershire sauce
⅛ teaspoon white pepper
¾ cup chopped tomato
½ cup finely shredded lettuce
½ cup julienned cooked turkey breast
½ cup julienned Swiss cheese
2 tablespoons sliced green onions
2 tablespoons quartered radish slices

• Completely dissolve gelatin and salt in boiling water. Combine cold water and enough ice cubes to measure 1¼ cups. Add to gelatin; stir until slightly thickened. Remove any unmelted ice. Stir in vinegar, dressing, Worcestershire sauce and pepper. Chill until slightly thickened.

• Stir remaining ingredients into gelatin mixture. Spoon into 2 individual plastic containers or serving dishes. Chill until firm, about 2 hours. Garnish, if desired.

Makes 3½ cups or 2 entrée servings

APRICOT AND PORK SALAD

¾ pound pork chops (about 2 small or 1 large)
1 quart torn assorted greens
¾ pound fresh ripe apricots, cut into wedges (5 or 6 apricots)
¾ cup walnut halves, toasted
½ cup vegetable oil
⅓ cup red wine vinegar
2 tablespoons sugar
¾ teaspoon tarragon, crumbled
¼ teaspoon marjoram, crumbled
¼ teaspoon thyme, crumbled

Broil pork chops for 5 to 6 minutes on each side or until done. (*Or*, if preferred, place pork in microwave-safe dish with ¼ inch water. Cover and cook at HIGH power for 3 to 5 minutes or until done; cool.) Cut cooked pork into narrow slivers. Place greens in salad bowl. Top with pork, apricots and walnuts. Combine oil, vinegar, sugar, tarragon, marjoram and thyme in small jar; shake well. Before serving, pour desired amount of dressing over salad. Refrigerate remaining dressing for later use.

Makes 2 servings

Favorite recipe from **California Apricot Advisory Board**

Chef's Salad

Buttermilk Pepper Dressing

BUTTERMILK PEPPER DRESSING

- **1 cup buttermilk**
- **½ cup MIRACLE WHIP® Salad Dressing**
- **2 tablespoons KRAFT® 100% Grated Parmesan Cheese**
- **1 teaspoon freshly ground pepper**
- **1 garlic clove, minced**

Mix together ingredients until well blended; chill. Serve with mixed greens salad.

Makes 1 cup

Prep time: 5 minutes plus chilling

TURKEY WALDORF SALAD

- **1 cup cooked rice (cooked in chicken broth), cooled**
- **1 cup cooked turkey breast strips**
- **¾ cup diced unpeeled apple**
- **½ cup sliced celery**
- **2 tablespoons slivered almonds, toasted**
- **3 tablespoons bottled poppy seed dressing**
- **Lettuce leaves**

Combine all ingredients except lettuce in medium bowl. Serve on lettuce.

Makes 2 servings

Favorite recipe from **USA Rice Council**

SHRIMP LOUIE

½ **head iceberg lettuce, shredded**
6 **ounces tiny cooked shrimp**
1 **can (8¼ ounces) DEL MONTE® Sliced Beets, drained**
1 **can (10½ ounces) DEL MONTE® Tender Green Asparagus Tips, drained**
1 **hard-cooked egg, sliced**
4 **ripe olives**
   Louie Dressing (recipe follows)

Place lettuce on two dinner plates. Place half of shrimp on each lettuce bed. Arrange beets, asparagus and egg around shrimp. Garnish with olives. Serve with Louie Dressing.

Makes 2 servings

LOUIE DRESSING

⅓ **cup mayonnaise**
¼ **cup DEL MONTE® Tomato Ketchup**
¼ **cup chopped green pepper**
2 **tablespoons chopped onion**
1 **tablespoon lemon juice**
½ **teaspooon Worcestershire sauce**

Place ingredients in blender container. Cover and blend until smooth. Chill several hours. Serve with Shrimp Louie. Remaining dressing may be refrigerated and served with other seafood or tossed green salads.

Makes approximately 1 cup

BAGEL PIZZA

2 **tablespoons prepared pizza sauce**
1 **bagel, cut in half**
2 **teaspoons grated Parmesan cheese**
2 **teaspoons sliced green onion**
2 **slices BORDEN® Lite-line® Mozzarella Flavor Process Cheese Product**
2 **teaspoons finely chopped green bell pepper**
2 **pitted ripe olives, sliced**

Preheat oven to 400°F. Spread 1 tablespoon pizza sauce on each bagel half. Top with equal portions of remaining ingredients. Place on baking sheet; bake at 400°F for 4 to 5 minutes *or* broil until Lite-line slice begins to melt. Garnish as desired.

Makes 1 serving

Bagel Pizza

CHICKEN "SATAY" SALAD

2 boneless, skinless chicken breast halves
1 tablespoon teriyaki sauce or glaze
1 teaspoon sesame oil
1 DOLE® Banana, peeled, sliced
1 small red bell pepper, sliced, seeded
½ DOLE® Fresh Pineapple, peeled, chunked
½ DOLE® Cantaloupe, peeled, chunked
   Crisp salad greens
2 tablespoons sliced green onion
1 tablespoon chopped peanuts

SATAY DRESSING
½ cup reduced-calorie dairy sour cream
3 tablespoons creamy peanut butter
2 tablespoons honey *or* brown sugar
1 tablespoon grated ginger root
1 tablespoon bottled hot salsa
1 large clove garlic, pressed
2 teaspoons soy sauce

Chicken "Satay" Salad

- Marinate chicken, covered and refrigerated, in combined teriyaki sauce and sesame oil 15 minutes or longer.

- Broil or grill chicken 15 to 20 minutes or until no longer pink in center, turning and basting occasionally. Slice chicken diagonally.

- On 2 plates, arrange chicken, banana, bell pepper, pineapple and melon on salad greens. Sprinkle with onion and peanuts. Serve with Satay Dressing.
  Makes 2 servings

SATAY DRESSING: In blender or food processor, combine all ingredients and blend until smooth.

Prep time: 20 minutes
Cook time: 15 minutes

BROILED CHEESE 'N TURKEY SANDWICH

1 cup chopped cooked BUTTERBALL® Turkey
¼ cup sliced pitted ripe olives
¼ cup mayonnaise
½ cup (2 ounces) shredded Cheddar cheese
4 slices pineapple, well drained
2 English muffins or sandwich buns, split and toasted

Preheat broiler. Combine turkey, olives, mayonnaise and cheese in small bowl. Place pineapple slices on muffin or bun halves. Spoon turkey mixture over pineapple slices. Arrange on broiler pan. Broil about 4 inches from heat until mixture is hot and cheese is bubbly.

Makes 2 servings
(4 open-faced sandwiches)

Beef, Tomato and Basil Salad

BEEF, TOMATO AND BASIL SALAD

**6 thin slices cooked beef eye
  round roast (about 6 ounces)**
12 fresh basil leaves
1 large tomato, cut into 6 slices
4 teaspoons *each:* **olive oil, red
  wine vinegar**
1 small clove garlic, minced
⅛ teaspoon salt
   Freshly ground black pepper

Place 2 basil leaves on each tomato slice. Arrange alternating slices of tomato/basil and cooked beef eye round roast on each of 2 dinner plates. Combine oil, vinegar, garlic and salt; drizzle over salad. Season with freshly ground pepper.

Makes 2 servings

Prep time: 8 to 10 minutes

Note: To prepare roast, place 2-pound beef eye round roast on rack in open roasting pan in a 325°F (slow) oven. Do not add water. Do not cover. Roast to 135°F. Allow approximately 20 to 22 minutes per pound. Roasts usually rise 5°F in temperature to reach 140°F for rare. A beef eye roast will yield four 3-ounce cooked servings per pound.

Favorite recipe from **National Live Stock and Meat Board**

COOL 'N' CRUNCHY LUNCHEON SALAD

¼ **cup mayonnaise**
¼ **teaspoon salt**
⅛ **teaspoon curry powder**
⅛ **teaspoon fresh lemon juice**
1 **cup cubed cooked turkey or chicken**
⅔ **cup nectarine slices**
¼ **cup celery slices**
3 **tablespoons chopped nuts**
1 **tablespoon chopped onion**

Combine mayonnaise, salt, curry powder and lemon juice in large bowl; mix well. Add remaining ingredients; mix lightly. Chill. Add additional mayonnaise just before serving, if desired. Garnish as desired.

Makes 2 servings

CITRUS, AVOCADO & BACON SALAD

3 **tablespoons orange juice concentrate, thawed**
2 **tablespoons vegetable oil**
1 **tablespoon lime juice**
1 **tablespoon honey**
1 **tablespoon white vinegar**
3 **cups mixed salad greens, washed and drained**
½ **avocado, peeled, pitted and sliced**
6 **slices ARMOUR® Lower Salt Bacon, cut in half and cooked crisp**
1 **(11-ounce) can mandarin oranges, drained**

Combine orange juice concentrate, oil, lime juice, honey and vinegar in small bowl; set aside. Divide mixed salad greens evenly between 2 individual salad plates. Arrange avocado and bacon spoke-fashion over greens. Arrange mandarin oranges on top of greens. Drizzle with dressing. Garnish with chopped unsalted peanuts, if desired.

Makes 2 servings

Cool 'n' Crunchy Luncheon Salad

Sesame Chicken in Pitas

SESAME CHICKEN IN PITAS

½ cup MIRACLE WHIP® FREE® Dressing
1 tablespoon *each*: soy sauce, toasted sesame seeds
1 teaspoon sesame oil (optional)
⅛ teaspoon ground ginger
1 cup chopped cooked chicken
½ cup *each*: chopped pea pods, chopped red bell pepper
¼ cup cashews
2 whole-wheat pita bread rounds, cut in half

- Mix dressing, soy sauce, sesame seeds, oil and ginger until well blended.

- Add chicken, vegetables and cashews; mix well. Spoon into pita pockets.

Makes 2 servings

TURKEY TOMATO MELTS

4 LOUIS RICH® Fresh Turkey Breast Slices (½ package)
1 tablespoon butter
4 slices tomato
4 green pepper rings
4 slices brick cheese, cut in half diagonally
4 slices French bread, toasted

Melt butter in skillet over medium heat. When butter begins to brown, add turkey. Cook 3 minutes; turn. Top with tomato, green pepper and cheese. Cover. Cook 2 minutes more. Serve open-faced on French bread.

Makes 2 servings

MARVELOUS MEATS

Nothing tantalizes the taste buds better than a succulent cut of meat. Page through this chapter for creative ways to use beef, pork, veal or lamb. You're sure to be impressed!

BEEF KABOBS OVER LEMON RICE

½ **pound boneless beef sirloin steak, cut in 1-inch cubes**
1 **small zucchini, sliced**
1 **small yellow squash, sliced**
1 **small red pepper, cut in squares**
1 **small onion, cut in chunks**
¼ **cup Italian dressing**
1 **cup hot cooked rice**
2 **teaspoons fresh lemon juice**
1 **tablespoon snipped fresh parsley**
¼ **teaspoon seasoned salt**

Combine beef and vegetables in plastic bag with zippered closing. Add dressing and marinate 4 to 6 hours in refrigerator. Alternate beef and vegetables on 4 skewers. Grill or broil, turning and basting with marinade, 5 to 7 minutes, or to desired doneness. Combine rice and remaining ingredients. Serve kabobs over rice mixture.

Makes 2 servings

Favorite recipe from **USA Rice Council**

STRAPPING SOUP

½ **pound ground round**
1 **tablespoon oil**
1 **teaspoon instant minced onion**
½ **cup water**
½ **(0.9-ounce) package dry vegetable soup mix**
½ **(15-ounce) can red kidney beans**
¾ **cup tomato juice**
¼ **teaspoon TABASCO® pepper sauce**

Sauté meat in oil until brown, breaking it into chunks. Stir in onion and add water. Heat to boiling. Add soup mix; cover. Cook for 10 minutes. Stir in beans, tomato juice and TABASCO®. Heat slowly to boiling.

Makes 2 servings

Beef Kabobs over Lemon Rice

FLANK STEAK TERIYAKI WITH SAVORY RICE

- ½ **cup peanut or vegetable oil**
- ¼ **cup dry red wine**
- 3 **tablespoons teriyaki sauce**
- 1 **jar (12 ounces) roasted red peppers, drained and chopped**
- 2 **tablespoons light brown sugar**
- 1 **tablespoon** *plus* **1 teaspoon finely chopped garlic**
- ⅛ **teaspoon crushed red pepper**
- ½ **pound beef flank steak, sliced diagonally into ¼-inch strips**
- 2 **tablespoons butter or margarine**
- 1 **teaspoon finely chopped fresh ginger (optional)**
- ½ **cup thinly sliced zucchini**
- 2 **cups water**
- 1 **package LIPTON® Rice & Sauce—Herb & Butter**
- **Black pepper, to taste**

In large shallow glass baking dish, thoroughly combine oil, wine, teriyaki sauce, 1 cup roasted peppers, brown sugar, 1 tablespoon garlic and crushed red pepper. Add steak and turn to coat. Cover and marinate in refrigerator, turning occasionally, at least 4 hours. Remove steak, reserving marinade.

Onto 4 large skewers, thread steak, weaving back and forth. Grill or broil, turning and basting with reserved marinade, 3 minutes or until done.

Meanwhile, in large skillet, melt butter and cook remaining 1 teaspoon garlic with ginger over medium-high heat 30 seconds. Add zucchini and cook, stirring frequently, 2 minutes or until tender. Stir in water and rice & herb & butter sauce and bring to a boil. Reduce heat and simmer, stirring occasionally, 10 minutes or until rice is tender. Stir in remaining roasted peppers and black pepper. Serve rice with steak.

Makes about 2 servings

Flank Steak Teriyaki with Savory Rice

EASY BEEF STROGANOFF

   2 **tablespoons oil**
   2 **teaspoons finely chopped garlic**
   ½ **pound boneless sirloin steak, cut into thin strips**
   ¼ **cup dry red wine**
   2 **teaspoons Worcestershire sauce**
1¼ **cups water**
   ½ **cup milk**
   2 **tablespoons butter or margarine**
   1 **package LIPTON® Noodles & Sauce—Stroganoff***
   ½ **cup pearl onions**

In large skillet, heat oil and cook garlic over medium heat 30 seconds. Add beef and cook over medium-high heat 1 minute or until almost done. Add wine and Worcestershire sauce and cook 30 seconds; remove beef. Into skillet, stir water, milk, butter and noodles & stroganoff sauce. Bring to the boiling point, then continue boiling, stirring occasionally, 7 minutes. Stir in onions and beef, then cook 2 minutes or until noodles are tender. Garnish, if desired, with chopped parsley and paprika.

Makes about 2 servings

*Also terrific with LIPTON® Noodles & Sauce—Beef Flavor

Pork Medallions with Dijon-Dill Sauce

PORK MEDALLIONS WITH DIJON-DILL SAUCE

   8 **ounces pork tenderloin**
   ½ **teaspoon garlic salt**
   ⅛ **teaspoon pepper**
   ¼ **cup plain yogurt**
   2 **teaspoons Dijon-style mustard**
   ¼ **teaspoon** *each*: **dill weed, sugar**

Cut pork crosswise into 4 pieces. To make medallions, place each piece of pork, cut side down, on flat surface; cover with waxed paper and flatten gently with heel of hand to ¼-inch thickness. Panbroil pork in nonstick frying pan over medium heat 3 to 4 minutes per side or until pork is done. Remove medallions to warm platter; season with garlic salt and pepper on both sides. Meanwhile, combine yogurt, mustard, dill weed and sugar. Serve with pork.

Makes 2 servings

Prep time: 15 minutes

Note: To serve sauce warm, place in heatproof measure and warm in hot (not boiling) water 2 to 3 minutes. Do not cook or let curdle.

Favorite recipe from **National Pork Producers Council**

AMERICA'S CUT WITH BALSAMIC VINEGAR

2 America's Cut (1½-inch-thick) boneless center pork loin chops
1½ teaspoons lemon pepper
1 teaspoon vegetable oil
3 tablespoons balsamic vinegar
2 tablespoons chicken broth
2 teaspoons butter

Pat chops dry. Coat with lemon pepper. Heat oil in heavy skillet over medium-high heat. Add chops. Brown on first side 8 minutes; turn and cook 7 minutes more or until done. Remove from pan and keep warm. Add vinegar and broth to skillet; cook, stirring, until syrupy (about 1 to 2 minutes). Stir in butter until blended. Spoon sauce over chops.

Makes 2 servings

Prep time: 20 minutes

Favorite recipe from **National Pork Producers Council**

SINGLE-PAN SPAGHETTI

⅓ pound ground round steak
1 tablespoon instant minced onion
1 jar (15½ ounces) spaghetti sauce with mushrooms
1¼ cups water
2 ounces uncooked spaghetti
½ cup (2 ounces) shredded Provolone or Mozzarella cheese
Grated Romano cheese

Combine ground round and minced onion; cook in medium skillet until meat is brown and crumbly. Stir in spaghetti sauce and water. Bring to boiling. Add spaghetti. Cover and simmer 25 to 30 minutes or until pasta is tender. Remove from heat and stir in Provolone cheese. Sprinkle each serving with Romano cheese. Serve immediately.

Makes 2 servings

Favorite recipe from **American Dairy Association**

HAM CARROT FETTUCCINI

1 cup *each*: sliced DOLE® Carrots, DOLE® Celery
1 cup DOLE® Asparagus tips *or* green beans
½ cup slivered smoked ham
1 large clove garlic, pressed
1 teaspoon Italian herbs
1 tablespoon *each*: margarine, olive oil
4 ounces fettuccini noodles, cooked
2 tablespoons grated Parmesan cheese

• Sauté vegetables, ham, garlic and herbs in margarine and oil 3 to 4 minutes or until tender-crisp.

• Stir in noodles until well mixed. Toss with cheese. Serve immediately.

Makes 2 servings

Prep time: 15 minutes
Cook time: 7 minutes

America's Cut with Balsamic Vinegar

HURRY-UP THURINGER AND BEAN SOUP

6 ounces fully-cooked smoked
    thuringer links, diagonally
    cut into ¼-inch slices
1 can (16 ounces) Great
    Northern beans, drained
1 small onion, quartered
1 clove garlic
1 cup single-strength beef broth
¼ cup dry sherry
¾ teaspoon ground cumin
1 tablespoon chopped parsley
    Lemon slices, if desired
    Dairy sour cream, if desired

Place beans, onion and garlic in
blender container or food
processor bowl fitted with steel
blade; process until smooth,
scraping side of bowl as
necessary. Add broth, sherry and
cumin; process until blended. Pour
mixture into a medium saucepan.
Bring to boil; reduce heat to
medium-low and cook, uncovered,
10 minutes, stirring occasionally.
Add sausage and continue cooking

Hurry-Up Thuringer and Bean Soup

10 minutes. Stir in parsley. Garnish
with lemon slices and sour cream,
if desired.

Makes 2 servings

Prep time: 10 minutes
Cook time: 20 minutes

Favorite recipe from **National Live Stock and
Meat Board**

MARDI GRAS BEEF BROIL

½ pound steak, 1 inch thick
½ teaspoon garlic powder
½ onion, cut in chunks
½ small green pepper, cut in
    strips
¼ teaspoon thyme, crushed
1 tablespoon oil
1 can (8 ounces) DEL MONTE®
    Original Style Stewed
    Tomatoes
1 teaspoon cornstarch

Sprinkle meat with ¼ teaspoon
garlic powder. Broil 5 inches from
heat, 6 to 8 minutes for medium
rare, or until cooked as desired,
turning once. In skillet, cook onion,
green pepper, thyme and remaining
¼ teaspoon garlic powder in oil
until vegetables are tender-crisp.
Drain tomatoes, reserving juice;
combine juice and cornstarch. Add
to vegetables; cook, stirring
constantly, until thickened. Add
tomatoes; heat thoroughly. Salt
and pepper to taste. Thinly slice
meat; top with vegetables.

Makes 2 servings

Variation: May substitute
DEL MONTE® Mexican Style
Stewed Tomatoes for Original
Style Tomatoes and ¼ teaspoon
oregano for thyme.

Southwestern Lamb Grill

SOUTHWESTERN LAMB GRILL

1 rack of American lamb, 8 ribs
3 tablespoons stone ground mustard
1 tablespoon Worcestershire sauce
½ teaspoon crushed red pepper
2 cloves garlic, minced

Trim all visible fat from rack. Stir together remaining ingredients. Spread on outside of lamb. If desired, for maximum flavor, lamb may be marinated for up to two days in refrigerator.

Outdoor grill method: Place lamb on grill, 6 to 8 inches from hot coals. Turn racks frequently, using tongs. Grill until thermometer registers 140°F for rare or 150°F for medium-rare.

Oven method: Place lamb on rack over broiler pan. Roast in preheated 325°F oven until meat thermometer registers 140°F for rare or 150°F for medium.

As an accompaniment, slice red or green peppers, zucchini, chile peppers and corn to desired size; brush with oil and sprinkle with chopped cilantro. Grill 6 to 8 inches over hot coals until tender.

Makes 2 servings

Favorite recipe from **American Lamb Council**

VEAL PICCATA

8 ounces veal cutlets, cut ⅛ to
   ¼ inch thick
4 teaspoons flour
¼ teaspoon salt
⅛ teaspoon freshly ground
   pepper
1 tablespoon olive oil
1 clove garlic, minced
¼ cup dry white wine
1 tablespoon fresh lemon juice
2 teaspoons capers, if desired

Place veal cutlets on flat surface;
cover with waxed paper and flatten
with bottom of saucepan, mallet or
cleaver to ⅛-inch thickness or
less. Combine flour, salt and
pepper; coat cutlets with flour
mixture. Immediately sauté cutlets
in hot oil in large nonstick frying
pan 1 to 1½ minutes, turning once.
Remove cutlets; keep warm. Add
garlic and cook 30 seconds,
stirring constantly. Add wine and
lemon juice; cook until slightly
reduced. Serve cutlets with sauce;
sprinkle with capers, if desired.

Makes 2 servings

Prep time: 10 minutes
Cook time: 3 minutes

Favorite recipe from **National Live Stock and
Meat Board**

VEGETABLE MEDLEY PASTA

3 ounces or 1½ cups uncooked
   bow tie pasta
¼ pound spicy Italian sausage
   links, sliced
1 cup sliced fresh mushrooms
1 can (8 ounces) DEL MONTE®
   Italian Style Stewed
   Tomatoes
1 can (8 ounces) DEL MONTE®
   Tomato Sauce
1 small carrot, diced
½ teaspoon basil, crushed
1 cup frozen chopped broccoli,
   thawed

Cook pasta as package directs;
drain. In skillet, brown sausage
with mushrooms over medium-
high heat; drain. Stir in tomatoes,
tomato sauce, carrot and basil.
Cook, uncovered, over medium
heat 10 to 12 minutes or until
thickened and vegetables are
tender. Stir in broccoli; heat
through. Serve immediately over
hot pasta. Garnish with grated
Parmesan cheese, if desired.

Makes 2 generous servings

Prep time: 5 minutes
Cook time: 20 minutes

Variation: Substitute fresh broccoli
for thawed frozen broccoli. Add
with tomatoes and carrots.

Veal Piccata

Pork Tenderloin with Gingersnap Gravy

PORK TENDERLOIN WITH GINGERSNAP GRAVY

1 whole pork tenderloin, about 12 ounces
2 tablespoons butter or margarine, divided
½ cup water
¼ cup sliced green onion
2 tablespoons chopped celery
1 clove garlic, minced
1 tablespoon cornstarch
½ teaspoon ground ginger
¼ teaspoon pepper
⅛ teaspoon dried thyme, crushed
Dash of rubbed sage

In a large skillet, melt 1 tablespoon butter. Add tenderloin and brown quickly on all sides. Remove from heat and gradually add water. Cover and cook over low heat for 30 to 45 minutes or until pork is done. Remove tenderloin; keep warm. Drain drippings into a 1-cup measure; set aside. In skillet, melt remaining 1 tablespoon butter. Add green onion, celery and garlic; sauté about 4 minutes or until crisp-tender.

Combine cornstarch, ginger, pepper, thyme and sage; mix well. Push vegetables to side of skillet; add cornstarch mixture, stirring until smooth. Add reserved drippings; cook over medium-high heat until thickened and bubbly.

To serve, slice pork and serve atop gravy.

Makes 2 servings

Prep time: 20 minutes
Cook time: 45 minutes

Favorite recipe from **National Pork Producers Council**

SHAPE-UP STEAK WITH STIR-FRIED SPINACH

1 beef top loin steak, cut 1 inch thick (about 8 ounces)
2 tablespoons reduced-sodium soy sauce
1 tablespoon dry sherry
2 teaspoons cornstarch
1 tablespoon dark sesame oil
⅛ to ¼ teaspoon crushed red pepper
1 small red bell pepper, cut into thin strips
½ pound (8 cups) fresh spinach leaves
1 cup fresh bean sprouts
1 teaspoon sesame seeds

Place beef top loin steak on rack in broiler pan so surface of meat is 3 to 4 inches from heat source. Broil to desired doneness (rare or medium), 15 to 20 minutes, turning once.

Meanwhile, heat wok or large heavy skillet over high heat. Combine soy sauce, sherry and cornstarch; reserve. Add oil and crushed red pepper to wok. Add red bell pepper strips; stir-fry 1 minute. Add spinach; toss until almost wilted. Add bean sprouts and reserved sauce; cook 1 minute until thickened, stirring constantly. Divide mixture evenly between 2 plates. Carve steak into ¼-inch slices. Arrange steak slices over vegetables; sprinkle with sesame seeds.

Makes 2 servings

Prep time: 10 minutes
Cook time: 15 to 20 minutes

Favorite recipe from **National Live Stock and Meat Board**

TASTY PORK RAGOUT

½ pound pork loin, cubed
1 small onion, chopped
1 large clove garlic, pressed
½ teaspoon rosemary, crumbled
2 tablespoons margarine
  Salt and pepper
1 bouillon cube
½ cup boiling water
2 cups DOLE® Cauliflower florettes
1 cup sliced DOLE® Carrots
1 cup hot cooked rice

• Brown pork with onion, garlic and rosemary in margarine. Season with salt and pepper to taste.

• Dissolve bouillon in water; stir into pork mixture. Cover; simmer 20 minutes.

• Add cauliflower and carrots. Cover; simmer 5 minutes longer or until tender-crisp. Serve with rice.

Makes 2 servings

Prep time: 10 minutes
Cook time: 25 minutes

Tasty Pork Ragout

ROLLED VEAL SURPRISE

1 cup chopped mushrooms
2 tablespoons butter or
   margarine
½ cup sliced green onions
1 package (10 ounces) frozen
   chopped spinach, defrosted
   and well drained
½ cup fresh bread crumbs
¼ cup chopped almonds
1 cup shredded Jarlsberg
   cheese
4 slices veal scallopini
   (about ½ pound)
6 slices bacon
2 tablespoons dry white wine
⅔ cup chicken broth or stock
1 tablespoon flour

In skillet, brown mushrooms in butter. Add green onions; sauté several minutes. Remove from heat. Blend in spinach, bread crumbs and almonds. Stir in cheese.

On waxed paper, lay out veal, slightly overlapping pieces to make 8×10-inch rectangle. Spread evenly with cheese mixture. Roll up jelly-roll fashion, using waxed paper to help, to make a 10-inch roll. Wrap in bacon and fasten with kitchen cord at 2-inch intervals. Place in shallow roasting pan.

Bake at 325°F for 30 minutes, or until veal is done. Remove veal from roasting pan. Heat drippings in pan over medium heat. Add wine; stir, gently scraping drippings off bottom of pan to deglaze. Blend together chicken broth and flour; add to pan. Cook, stirring occasionally, until thickened. Slice veal and arrange on platter. Spoon sauce over veal.

Makes 2 generous servings

Note: If desired, serve with cooked orzo or rice. Garnish with fresh basil leaves or parsley.

Favorite recipe from **Norseland Foods, Inc.**

ORIENTAL PEPPER STEAK

1 tablespoon oil
½ pound boneless chuck steak,
   cut into thin strips
2 envelopes LIPTON® Onion
   Cup-a-Soup
¼ teaspoon garlic powder
1 cup water
1 large green pepper, cut into
   thin strips
1 large tomato, cut into wedges
1½ teaspoons cornstarch

In small skillet, heat oil and brown beef; drain. Stir in instant onion soup mix and garlic powder blended with ¾ cup water. Simmer, covered, 15 minutes. Add green pepper and tomato; simmer, covered, an additional 15 minutes or until beef is tender. Stir in cornstarch blended with remaining ¼ cup water. Bring to a boil, then simmer, stirring constantly, until sauce is thickened, about 5 minutes. Serve, if desired, over hot cooked rice.

Makes about 2 servings

PORK SMITTANE

2 **butterfly pork chops, cut**
½ inch thick
3 **tablespoons all-purpose flour**
¼ **teaspoon pepper**
2 **teaspoons butter or margarine**
1 **tablespoon finely chopped**
green onion
⅓ **cup dry white wine**
1 **teaspoon Dijon-style mustard**
¼ **cup cold water**
1½ **teaspoons all-purpose flour**

Pound pork with a meat mallet to ¼-inch thickness. Combine 3 tablespoons flour and pepper; dredge chops lightly in flour mixture. In a medium skillet, melt butter; add chops and brown on both sides. Remove chops and set aside.

Add green onion to drippings; cook over medium heat until crisp-tender. Stir in wine and mustard. Return chops to skillet. Cover and reduce heat to medium-low. Simmer for 15 to 18 minutes or until done. Remove chops and set aside.

Combine water and 1½ teaspoons flour, mixing until well blended. Add flour mixture to drippings. Cook over medium-high heat until thickened and bubbly, stirring constantly. Return chops to skillet. Cover and cook for 2 to 3 minutes or until heated through.

Makes 2 servings

Prep time: 30 minutes

Favorite recipe from **National Pork Producers Council**

Pork Smittane

PREMIER POULTRY

As chicken and turkey continue to grow in popularity, so does the search for imaginative ways to prepare them. From "Chicken Scaparella" to "Quesadilla Grande," you're sure to discover new favorites here.

CHICKEN SCAPARELLA

- 2 slices bacon, coarsely chopped
- 2 tablespoons FILIPPO BERIO® Olive Oil
- 1 large chicken breast, split
- ½ cup quartered mushrooms
- 1 small clove garlic, minced
- 1 cup plus 2 tablespoons chicken broth
- 2 tablespoons red wine vinegar
- 8 small white onions, peeled
- 4 small new potatoes, halved
- ½ teaspoon salt
- ⅛ teaspoon pepper
- 2 tablespoons flour
  Chopped parsley

In skillet, cook bacon. Remove and set aside. Add oil and chicken. Brown well on all sides. Add mushrooms and garlic. Sauté several minutes, stirring occasionally. Add 1 cup chicken broth and next 5 ingredients. Cover and simmer 35 minutes until chicken and vegetables are tender.

To thicken sauce, dissolve 1 tablespoon flour in 2 tablespoons chicken broth. Stir into sauce. Cook, stirring, until thickened and smooth. Garnish with parsley.

Makes 2 servings

TURKEY PARMESAN

- 1 teaspoon diet margarine
- 1 (2-ounce) slice fresh turkey breast
- 3 tablespoons prepared pasta sauce
- 1 tablespoon grated Parmesan cheese
- 1 slice BORDEN® Lite-line® Process Cheese Product, any flavor

In small skillet, over medium heat, melt margarine. Add turkey breast slice. Cook 2 minutes; turn. Reduce heat to low; top turkey with remaining ingredients. Cover; cook 2 to 3 minutes longer or until turkey is no longer pink. Garnish as desired.

Makes 1 serving

Chicken Scaparella

Turkey Normande

TURKEY NORMANDE

**1 package (about 2 pounds)
LOUIS RICH® Fresh Turkey
Drumsticks**

**SAUCE
1 cup apple butter
2 tablespoons soy sauce**

Rinse turkey. Wrap each drumstick in heavy-duty foil. Cook 45 minutes in covered kettle grill, 4 inches from medium-hot coals; turn. Cook 45 minutes more. (Add coals during cooking to maintain heat.) Meanwhile, combine sauce ingredients. Remove turkey from foil. Brush with sauce and grill 10 minutes more or until turkey is no longer pink in center, turning occasionally. Heat remaining sauce and serve with turkey.

Makes 2 generous servings

To Make Ahead: Rinse turkey. Place in skillet with 1 cup water. Bring to a boil; reduce heat. Cover. Simmer 2 hours. Pour off liquid. Cover and refrigerate. Before serving, grill turkey 4 inches from medium-hot coals 30 minutes, turning occasionally. Brush with sauce and grill 10 minutes more.

CHICKEN AND VEGETABLE STEW

This stew for two takes just minutes to prepare.

- **1 package (1.50 ounces) LAWRY'S® Extra Rich & Thick Spaghetti Sauce Spices & Seasonings**
- **1 can (6 ounces) tomato paste**
- **1¾ cups water**
- **2 tablespoons vegetable oil**
- **1 whole chicken breast, boned and cut into bite-size pieces**
- **½ teaspoon LAWRY'S® Garlic Salt**
- **2 cups thinly sliced zucchini**
- **2 cups thinly sliced fresh mushrooms**
- **½ cup thinly sliced onion, separated into rings**
- **1 can (2.25 ounces) sliced ripe olives, drained**
- **Hot cooked pasta**
- **Parmesan cheese**

Prepare Extra Rich & Thick Spaghetti Sauce Spices & Seasonings with tomato paste, water and oil according to package directions; set aside. In 1½-quart casserole dish, arrange chicken and sprinkle with Garlic Salt. Top with zucchini, mushrooms, onion and olives. Pour spaghetti sauce over. Bake, uncovered, in 350°F oven 30 minutes.

Makes 2 servings

Note: Serve over the pasta of your choice with Parmesan cheese (freshly grated preferred) for topping.

CHICKEN PAPRIKA

- **¾ cup vegetable juice**
- **1½ teaspoons flour**
- **2 teaspoons paprika**
- **½ teaspoon seasoned salt**
- **1 teaspoon olive oil**
- **¼ cup sliced green onions, including tops**
- **1 clove garlic, minced**
- **½ pound boneless chicken breasts, cut in 2-inch strips**
- **2 tablespoons dairy sour cream**
- **1 cup hot cooked rice**

Combine vegetable juice, flour, paprika and salt in small bowl; set aside. Heat oil in medium skillet over medium heat. Add onions and garlic; cook 1 minute. Add chicken strips; cook until chicken is lightly browned. Add vegetable juice mixture. Cook until mixture boils, stirring often. Reduce heat to low; cover and simmer 15 minutes. Remove from heat; stir in sour cream. Serve over rice. Garnish with snipped fresh parsley, if desired.

Makes 2 servings

MICROWAVE: Combine vegetable juice, flour, paprika and salt in small bowl; set aside. Combine oil, onions and garlic in medium microproof baking dish. Cover and cook on HIGH (maximum power) 1 minute. Add chicken strips and cook on HIGH 1 minute. Stir and cook 1 additional minute or until chicken loses its pink color. Add vegetable juice mixture; cover and cook on HIGH 2 to 3 minutes or until mixture boils. Stir; cover and cook on MEDIUM-LOW (30% power) 15 minutes. Remove from oven and stir in sour cream. Serve over rice. Garnish as directed.

Favorite recipe from **USA Rice Council**

GRILLED CHICKEN SKEWERS

½ **pound boneless, skinless chicken breasts, cut into thin strips**
½ **pound bacon slices**
⅓ **cup lemon juice**
⅓ **cup honey**
1½ **teaspoons LAWRY'S® Lemon Pepper Seasoning**
½ **teaspoon LAWRY'S® Seasoned Salt**

Thread chicken strips and bacon slices onto wooden skewers. In shallow dish, combine remaining ingredients. Add prepared skewers; cover and refrigerate 1 hour or overnight. Grill or broil 10 to 15 minutes, basting with marinade, until chicken is cooked through and bacon is crisp.

Makes 2 servings

Hints:
Soak wooden skewers in water before adding chicken and bacon to prevent skewers from burning.

Do not baste chicken with marinade during last 5 minutes of cooking.

QUICK SWEET AND SOUR CHICKEN

½ **package (10 to 12 ounces) frozen breaded chicken chunks**
1 **can (8¾ ounces) apricot halves in syrup, drained**
1 **package (8 ounces) frozen sugar snap peas**
2 **tablespoons bottled sweet and sour sauce**
1 **teaspoon soy sauce**
1 **cup hot cooked rice**

Bake chicken chunks according to package directions. Meanwhile, heat apricots, snap peas, sweet and sour sauce and soy sauce in medium saucepan over medium heat until peas are tender-crisp. Stir chicken into apricot mixture. Serve chicken mixture over rice.

Makes 2 servings

MICROWAVE: Microwave chicken chunks according to package directions; keep warm. Combine apricots, snap peas, sweet and sour sauce and soy sauce in medium microproof baking dish. Cover and cook on HIGH (maximum power) 2 minutes; stir. Cook on HIGH an additional 1 to 2 minutes or until thoroughly heated. Stir chicken into apricot mixture. Serve chicken mixture over rice.

Favorite recipe from **USA Rice Council**

Grilled Chicken Skewers

TURKEY MEDALLIONS WITH CUMBERLAND SAUCE

2½ teaspoons margarine
¼ cup currant jelly
1½ tablespoons Port wine
¾ teaspoon prepared mustard
2 teaspoons lemon juice
Dash of cayenne pepper
1 teaspoon cornstarch
2 teaspoons cold water
1 Turkey Tenderloin (½ pound)
Salt and black pepper, to taste
1 tablespoon olive oil

1. In small saucepan, over medium-high heat, melt 1 teaspoon margarine. Stir in jelly, wine, mustard, lemon juice and cayenne pepper; heat until jelly is melted.

2. In small bowl, combine cornstarch and water. Stir into jelly mixture. Boil mixture until thickened. Reduce heat and keep warm.

3. Cut tenderloin into ¾-inch-thick crosswise slices to make medallions. Season with salt and black pepper.

4. In a large skillet, over medium-high heat, sauté medallions in olive oil and remaining 1½ teaspoons margarine about 2½ minutes per side, or until no longer pink in thickest part of meat.

5. To serve, spoon a thin layer of sauce on center of each plate. Arrange several turkey medallions over sauce. Garnish with sour cream and fresh chives, if desired.

Makes 2 servings

Favorite recipe from **National Turkey Federation**

Turkey Medallions with Cumberland Sauce

Chicken Rosemary

CHICKEN ROSEMARY

2 boneless, skinless chicken
　　breast halves
1 teaspoon margarine
1 teaspoon olive oil
　　Salt and pepper
1 large clove garlic, minced
½ small onion, sliced
½ teaspoon rosemary, crumbled
⅛ teaspoon ground cinnamon
½ cup DOLE® Pine-Orange-
　　Guava Juice
1 tablespoon orange marmalade
2 cups sliced DOLE® Carrots

• Pound chicken to ½-inch thickness. Brown chicken in margarine and oil on both sides. Sprinkle with salt and pepper.

• Stir in garlic, onion, rosemary and cinnamon. Cook until onion is soft.

• Blend in juice and marmalade. Spoon over chicken. Cover; simmer 10 minutes.

• Stir in carrots. Cover; simmer 5 minutes or until tender-crisp.
　　　　　　　　Makes 2 servings

Prep time: 10 minutes
Cook time: 20 minutes

Turkey-Olive Ragout en Crust

TURKEY-OLIVE RAGOUT EN CRUST

½ **pound Boneless White or Dark Turkey Meat, cut into 1-inch cubes**
1 **clove garlic, minced**
1 **teaspoon vegetable oil**
¼ **cup (about 10) small whole frozen onions**
½ **cup reduced-sodium chicken bouillon or turkey broth**
½ **teaspoon dried parsley flakes**
⅛ **teaspoon dried thyme**
1 **small bay leaf**
1 **medium red potato, skin on, cut into ½-inch cubes**
10 **frozen snow peas**
8 **whole, small pitted black olives**
1 **can (4 ounces) refrigerator crescent rolls**
½ **teaspoon dried dill weed**

1. Preheat oven to 375°F.

2. In medium skillet over medium heat, sauté turkey in garlic and oil 3 to 4 minutes or until no longer pink; remove and set aside. Add onions to skillet and sauté until lightly browned. Add bouillon, parsley, thyme, bay leaf and potatoes. Bring mixture to a boil. Reduce heat; cover and simmer 10 minutes or until potatoes are tender. Remove bay leaf.

3. Combine turkey with potato mixture. Fold in snow peas and olives. Divide mixture between 2 (1¾-cup) casseroles.

4. Divide crescent rolls into 2 rectangles; press perforations together to seal. If necessary, roll out each rectangle to make dough large enough to cover top

of casserole. Sprinkle dough with dill weed, pressing lightly into dough. Cut small decorative shape from each dough piece; discard or place on baking sheet and bake in oven with casseroles. Place dough over turkey-vegetable mixture; trim dough to fit. Press dough to edge of casserole to seal. Bake 7 to 8 minutes or until pastry is golden brown.

Makes 2 servings

Lattice Crust: With a pastry wheel or knife, cut each rectangle into 6 lengthwise strips. Arrange strips, lattice-fashion, over turkey-vegetable mixture; trim dough to fit. Press ends of dough to edge of casserole to seal.

Note: For a more golden crust, brush top of dough with beaten egg yolk before baking.

Favorite recipe from **National Turkey Federation**

LITE-STUFFED CHICKEN BREASTS

2 skinned boneless chicken breast halves
2 tablespoons soy sauce
1 tablespoon diet margarine
1 tablespoon REALEMON® Lemon Juice from Concentrate
½ teaspoon thyme leaves
2 slices BORDEN® Lite-line® Process Cheese Product, each cut lengthwise into 3 equal strips
Chopped parsley, optional

Preheat oven to 375°F. Cut a 1½-inch pocket lengthwise in the thick side of each breast. In small saucepan, heat soy sauce, margarine, ReaLemon® brand and thyme. Place chicken in shallow baking dish; pour sauce over. Bake 25 to 30 minutes or until tender, basting occasionally with sauce. Remove from oven; place 3 strips Lite-line product in each pocket. Return to oven 5 minutes or until Lite-line product melts. Sprinkle with parsley, if desired. Serve immediately. Refrigerate leftovers.

Makes 2 servings

TEX-MEX TURKEY CASSEROLE

½ pound Ground Turkey
¼ cup onion, chopped
1 clove garlic, minced
¼ cup green pepper, chopped
½ teaspoon chili powder
½ cup chunky salsa
⅓ cup no-salt corn chips, crushed
2 tablespoons shredded reduced-calorie Cheddar cheese

1. Preheat oven to 350°F.

2. In medium nonstick skillet, over medium-high heat, sauté turkey, onion, garlic, green pepper and chili powder 3 to 5 minutes, or until turkey is no longer pink. Remove meat mixture from heat; stir in salsa.

3. Spread mixture into a 2¾-cup casserole dish; top with corn chips. Bake 10 minutes. Sprinkle with cheese and bake 5 minutes or until cheese melts.

Makes 2 servings

Favorite recipe from **National Turkey Federation**

QUESADILLA GRANDE

2 flour tortillas, 8-inch diameter
2 to 3 large fresh spinach leaves, stems removed, rinsed and patted dry
2 to 3 slices cooked chicken breast
2 tablespoons salsa
1 tablespoon chopped cilantro leaves
¼ cup (1 ounce) shredded Monterey Jack cheese
2 teaspoons butter or margarine (optional)

Place 1 tortilla in large nonstick skillet; cover tortilla with spinach leaves. Place chicken in single layer over spinach. Spoon salsa over chicken. Sprinkle with cilantro; top with cheese. Place remaining tortilla on top, pressing tortilla down so filling becomes compact.

Cook over medium heat 4 to 5 minutes or until bottom tortilla is lightly browned. Holding top tortilla in place, gently turn over. Continue cooking 4 minutes or until bottom tortilla is browned and cheese is melted. For a crispy finish, add butter to skillet to melt; lift quesadilla to let butter flow into center of skillet. Cook 30 seconds. Turn over; continue cooking 30 seconds. Cut into wedges to serve.

Makes 1 serving

Note: Recipe may be doubled.

THAI FOR TWO

1 tablespoon vegetable oil
1 tablespoon soy sauce
1 clove garlic, finely chopped *or* ⅛ teaspoon garlic powder
½ teaspoon ground ginger *or* ¼ teaspoon grated fresh ginger
¼ teaspoon crushed red pepper flakes
8 ounces LOUIS RICH®, fully cooked, Honey Roasted Breast of Turkey, cut into 4 (¼-inch-thick) slices
1½ cups water
1 tablespoon lime juice
2 cups uncooked instant rice
½ cucumber, peeled and sliced
2 green onions with tops, sliced
½ red bell pepper, sliced (optional)

• Mix oil, soy sauce, garlic and seasonings in small bowl; set aside.

• Place turkey in skillet. Pour sauce evenly over turkey.

• Heat turkey; add water and lime juice to skillet. Bring to a boil. Stir in rice; arrange turkey on top. Cover. Remove skillet from heat. Let stand, covered, 5 minutes.

• Fluff rice with fork; top with cucumber, green onions and red pepper slices before serving.

Makes 2 generous servings

Quesadilla Grande

CANCUN CHICKEN

1 large DOLE® Fresh Pineapple
2 boneless, skinless chicken
   breast halves
   Salt and pepper, to taste
½ teaspoon ground cumin
¼ teaspoon oregano, crumbled
⅛ teaspoon ground cloves
1 tablespoon olive oil
¾ cup DOLE® Pineapple Juice
1 tablespoon lime juice
1 teaspoon cornstarch
1 teaspoon minced cilantro

- Twist crown from pineapple. Cut pineapple lengthwise in half. Cut fruit from shells with a knife. Refrigerate half for later use. Cut remaining fruit crosswise into 6 slices.

- Pound chicken to ½-inch thickness. Sprinkle with salt and pepper. Combine cumin, oregano and cloves. Sprinkle over chicken.

- Heat olive oil in skillet. Lightly sauté pineapple about 1 minute. Remove from skillet.

- Brown chicken in pan juices. Cover; simmer 1 to 2 minutes until done.

- Combine pineapple juice, lime juice and cornstarch. Pour into skillet. Cook, stirring, until sauce boils and thickens. Stir in cilantro. Serve sauce over chicken and pineapple.

Makes 2 servings

Prep time: 15 minutes
Cook time: 10 minutes

Cancun Chicken

TURKEY AND VEGGIES IN CREAMY DILL SAUCE

½ pound Turkey Cutlets, cut into
   ½-inch strips
1 package (8 ounces) frozen
   mixed broccoli and
   cauliflower florets and carrot
   slices
1 tablespoon margarine
½ teaspoon dill weed
¼ teaspoon salt
⅛ teaspoon pepper
½ cup plain low-fat yogurt

1. In a 10-inch skillet, over medium-high heat, sauté turkey and frozen vegetables in margarine for 4 minutes.

2. Stir in dill, salt and pepper. Cover; reduce heat to low and cook 6 minutes or until vegetables are fork tender and turkey is no longer pink.

3. Remove from heat; stir in yogurt. Return skillet to low heat for approximately 1 minute to heat mixture throughout.

Makes 2 servings

Favorite recipe from **National Turkey Federation**

1 POTATO . . .

- **1 large Idaho potato, about 8 ounces**
- **½ cup cottage cheese**
- **¼ cup diced smoked turkey breast**
- **2 tablespoons shredded carrot**
- **1 tablespoon *each*: chopped green pepper, green onion**
- **½ teaspoon Worcestershire sauce**
- **⅛ teaspoon black pepper**

Preheat oven to 400°F. Pierce potato with a fork in several places. Bake about 50 minutes or until tender. Meanwhile, beat cottage cheese in small mixing bowl until fairly smooth. Stir in remaining ingredients. Split potato and top with cottage cheese mixture. Serve immediately.

Makes 1 serving

Favorite recipe from **American Dairy Association**

TURKEY À L'ORANGE

- **1 package (about 1 pound) LOUIS RICH® Fresh Turkey Tenderloins**
- **1 tablespoon firmly packed brown sugar**
- **2 teaspoons cornstarch**
- **½ cup orange juice**
- **1½ teaspoons lemon juice**
- **1 teaspoon butter**
- **1 tablespoon brandy, optional**

Place turkey on broiler pan. Position oven rack so top of turkey is 5 inches from heat source. Broil 10 minutes; turn. Broil 10 minutes more. Meanwhile, combine sugar and cornstarch in saucepan; add

Turkey à l'Orange

juices and butter. Cook on medium, stirring constantly, until thickened. Serve over turkey.

Makes 2 generous servings

To flame: Heat brandy in small pan over low heat until it begins to sizzle along the sides of pan when tilted. Remove from heat. Using a long match, light brandy; pour over turkey and sauce.

MICROWAVE: Place turkey in glass baking dish; cover with plastic wrap, turning back corner to vent. Microwave at HIGH 4 minutes. Turn turkey over. Cover. Microwave at HIGH 2 to 5 minutes more until no longer pink. Combine sugar, cornstarch, juices and butter in 2-cup glass measure. Microwave at HIGH 2 minutes, stirring halfway through cooking. Serve over turkey.

Note: Recipe is written for large (2 per package) turkey breast tenderloins. Decrease total cooking time 10 minutes if small (3 or 4 per package) tenderloins are used.

TURKEY AND FRUIT SKILLET DELIGHT

¼ teaspoon salt
⅛ teaspoon cinnamon
   Dash of cloves
   Dash of nutmeg
½ pound Turkey Cutlets, cut into
   1 × ¼-inch strips
1½ teaspoons margarine
⅓ cup mixed dried fruit*
1 cup apple juice
1 teaspoon cornstarch

1. In a small dish, combine salt, cinnamon, cloves and nutmeg. Dredge turkey in mixture to coat.

2. In a 10-inch nonstick skillet, over medium-high heat, sauté turkey in margarine until meat is no longer pink. Add mixed fruit and ½ cup apple juice; cover. Reduce heat to low and cook 15 minutes or until fruit is soft.

3. In a small bowl, combine cornstarch and remaining ½ cup juice. Add to meat mixture. Increase heat to medium and cook until sauce is thickened.

4. Serve over rice, if desired.

Makes 2 servings

*Cut large pieces of fruit in half and pit prunes, if necessary.

Favorite recipe from **National Turkey Federation**

ZESTY PASTA WITH RICOTTA

¾ cup lowfat Ricotta cheese
3 tablespoons plain lowfat yogurt
¼ teaspoon *each*: salt, pepper, garlic powder, nutmeg
⅓ cup sliced fresh mushrooms
¼ cup shredded carrot
3 tablespoons sliced green onion
1 tablespoon butter
½ (10-ounce) package frozen chopped spinach, thawed and well drained
4 ounces cubed cooked chicken* (about ½ cup)
2 ounces dried thin spaghetti
2 tablespoons grated Parmesan cheese

Beat Ricotta cheese in small mixer bowl until creamy, about 3 minutes. Beat in yogurt, seasonings and nutmeg until blended; set aside. Meanwhile, sauté mushrooms, carrot and onion in butter until tender-crisp, about 3 minutes. Combine cheese mixture, sautéed vegetables, spinach and chicken; set aside. Cook spaghetti according to package directions; rinse and drain. Quickly toss hot pasta with cheese-vegetable mixture. Divide evenly between 2 plates. Sprinkle each serving with 1 tablespoon Parmesan cheese. Serve immediately.

Makes 2 servings

*Cooked chicken breast, available at most deli counters, may be used.

Favorite recipe from **American Dairy Association**

CORNISH HENS WITH FRUITY PILAF STUFFING

¼ **cup Dijon-style mustard**
2 **tablespoons honey**
¾ **teaspoon curry powder**
1¼ **cups water**
1 **can (5½ ounces) apricot nectar**
2 **tablespoons butter or margarine**
½ **cup dried apricots, chopped**
1 **package LIPTON® Rice & Sauce—Pilaf**
½ **cup sliced green onions**
¼ **cup chopped walnuts**
2 **Cornish hens (1 to 1½ pounds each)**

Preheat oven to 375°F.

In small bowl, thoroughly blend mustard, honey and ¼ teaspoon curry powder.

In medium saucepan, bring water, nectar and butter to a boil. Add apricots and cook 1 minute. Stir in rice & pilaf sauce and remaining ½ teaspoon curry powder, then simmer, stirring occasionally, 10 minutes or until rice is tender. Stir in green onions and walnuts; let cool slightly. Stuff hens with rice mixture; secure cavities with skewers or wooden toothpicks, then tie legs together with string. In roasting pan, on rack, arrange hens. Roast, basting occasionally, with mustard mixture, 1 hour or until meat thermometer reaches 185°F. Bake any remaining stuffing in covered casserole during last 20 minutes of cooking time.

Makes 2 servings

TURKEY CASHEW CUTLETS

⅛ **teaspoon pepper**
½ **pound Turkey Breast Cutlets or Slices**
2 **ounces Swiss cheese, sliced**
2 **teaspoons seasoned bread crumbs**
2 **tablespoons white wine Worcestershire sauce**
1 **tablespoon cashews, coarsely chopped**

1. Preheat oven to 375°F.

2. Lightly sprinkle pepper over cutlets. Place a cheese slice on each cutlet. Roll up cutlets, jelly-roll style, to encase cheese.

3. Carefully coat each cutlet roll in bread crumbs.

4. In a 14-ounce oval casserole dish, arrange cutlet rolls, seam sides down. Spoon Worcestershire sauce over cutlets. Bake 10 minutes.

5. Baste cutlets with pan drippings. Sprinkle cashews over top. Bake 5 minutes or until turkey is no longer pink in center.

Makes 2 servings

Favorite recipe from **National Turkey Federation**

FROM THE SEA

Make a fish lover out of anyone with this dazzling sampler of recipes from the sea. Choose "Shrimp Diane," "Rainbow Trout Parmesan" or "Salmon with Chive Sauce"—no one will be disappointed!

FESTIVAL SHRIMP AND SAFFRON RICE

- ⅓ **cup diced red pepper**
- ¼ **cup sliced green onions, including tops**
- 1 **clove garlic, minced**
- 1 **teaspoon butter or margarine**
- ½ **pound peeled and deveined medium shrimp**
- ½ **teaspoon seafood seasoning blend**
- 1½ **cups cooked rice (cooked with ¹⁄₁₆ teaspoon ground saffron *or* turmeric)**
- 1 **tablespoon grated Parmesan cheese**

Cook pepper, onions and garlic in butter in medium skillet over medium heat 1 to 2 minutes. Add shrimp and seasoning blend; cook, stirring, 3 to 4 minutes. Stir in rice and cheese; cook and stir until thoroughly heated (about 2 to 3 minutes).

Makes 2 servings

MICROWAVE: Combine pepper, onions, garlic and butter in 1-quart microproof baking dish. Cover and cook on HIGH (maximum power) 2 minutes. Add shrimp and seasoning blend. Reduce setting to MEDIUM HIGH (70% power); cover and cook 3 to 4 minutes or until shrimp are opaque. Stir in rice and cheese; cover and cook on MEDIUM HIGH 1 to 2 minutes or until thoroughly heated. Let stand 2 minutes.

Favorite recipe from **USA Rice Council**

Festival Shrimp and Saffron Rice

TUNA AU GRATIN FOR TWO

- 1 cup sliced mushrooms
- ¼ cup sliced green onions
- ¼ teaspoon dill weed
- 2 tablespoons butter or margarine
- Grated peel and juice of ½ fresh lemon
- 1 can (7½ ounces) semi-condensed cream of mushroom soup with wine
- 1 can (7 ounces) solid-pack tuna, drained, chunked
- 2 tablespoons sliced canned pimiento
- 1 package (10 ounces) frozen broccoli spears, cooked, drained
- 2 to 3 tablespoons grated Parmesan cheese
- Lemon slices for garnish

In saucepan, sauté mushrooms and green onions with dill weed in butter until just tender. Stir in lemon peel, juice, soup, tuna and pimiento; heat. Arrange broccoli spears in 2 small oven-proof au gratin or baking dishes. Spoon tuna mixture over broccoli. Sprinkle with Parmesan cheese. Broil 4 to 5 minutes or bake at 400°F for 8 to 10 minutes until heated through. Garnish with lemon slices.

Makes 2 servings

Variation: Substitute 10¾-ounce can condensed cream of mushroom soup for semi-condensed cream of mushroom soup with wine.

Favorite recipe from **Sunkist Growers, Inc.**

Tuna au Gratin for Two

QUICK MEDITERRANEAN FISH

½ medium onion, sliced
1 tablespoon olive oil
1 small clove garlic, crushed
1 can (8 ounces) DEL MONTE® Italian Style Stewed Tomatoes
2 tablespoons medium green chile salsa
⅛ teaspoon cinnamon
¾ pound firm fish (halibut, salmon, red snapper or sea bass)
6 stuffed green olives, halved crosswise

In 1½-quart microwavable dish, combine onion, oil and garlic. Cover and microwave on HIGH 2 to 3 minutes or until onion is tender; drain. Stir in tomatoes, salsa and cinnamon. Top with fish and olives. Cover and microwave on HIGH 3 to 4 minutes or until fish flakes with fork.

Makes 2 servings

Variation: May substitute DEL MONTE® Original Style Stewed Tomatoes for Italian Style Tomatoes.

BLACK BEAN SAUCED SEAFOOD

3 tablespoons Chinese fermented black beans* (*dow shih*)
¾ cup chicken broth *or* water
2 tablespoons light soy sauce
2 tablespoons dry sherry
2 teaspoons cornstarch
1 teaspoon sugar
4 thin slices ginger root
1 clove garlic, crushed
8 ounces Surimi Seafood, crab flavored, chunk or leg style, cut diagonally
Cooked brown or white rice
2 green onions, thinly sliced

Rinse salt from black beans; soak briefly in water to cover.

Meanwhile, in blender container, combine chicken broth, soy sauce, sherry, cornstarch, sugar, ginger root and garlic. Drain black beans; add to container. Cover and blend, pulsing motor, until smooth.

Pour mixture into small saucepan; cook over medium heat, stirring constantly, for 3 to 5 minutes or until sauce is thickened. Stir in surimi. Reduce heat to low; cover. Simmer 2 to 3 minutes or until surimi is thoroughly heated. Serve over rice. Sprinkle with green onions.

Makes 2 servings

*Available at Oriental markets.

Favorite recipe from **National Fisheries Institute**

Halibut Marengo

HALIBUT MARENGO

**2 North Pacific halibut steaks
(¾ to 1 pound)
Grated peel and juice of
½ fresh lemon
1 medium tomato, diced
¼ cup chopped green pepper
2 tablespoons finely chopped
onion
1 tablespoon chopped parsley
1 clove garlic, minced
¼ teaspoon oregano leaves,
crushed
¼ teaspoon salt
⅛ teaspoon pepper
1 tablespoon olive oil
Lemon cartwheel twists**

Place halibut steaks in oiled
shallow baking dish or oven-proof
skillet. Sprinkle with lemon peel
and juice. Combine vegetables and
seasonings; spoon over halibut.
Drizzle with olive oil. Cover and
bake at 350°F, 25 to 30 minutes,
until fish flakes easily with fork.
Garnish with lemon cartwheel
twists.

Makes 2 servings

Favorite recipe from **Sunkist Growers, Inc.**

MICROWAVED SALMON STEAKS WITH MUSHROOMS

**2 tablespoons white wine
vinegar
1 tablespoon olive oil or
vegetable oil
½ teaspoon dried basil, crushed
⅛ teaspoon pepper
2 salmon steaks, about
6 ounces each (or 1 large
salmon steak, split)
¼ pound (4 large) thinly sliced
mushrooms
¼ cup thinly sliced green onions**

Combine vinegar, oil, basil and
pepper in 8×8-inch glass dish. Add
salmon; turn to coat both sides.
Marinate 15 to 30 minutes, turning
once. Drain marinade into 4-cup
glass measure. Add mushrooms
and green onions; stir to coat well.
Place salmon in glass dish. Cover
with waxed paper. Microwave at
HIGH 4 minutes, turning dish once;
let stand, covered, 3 minutes. (Fish
is done when it begins to flake
easily when tested with a fork.)
Microwave mushroom mixture,
uncovered, at HIGH 3 minutes,
stirring once. Transfer salmon to
hot plates; spoon mushroom
mixture over top.

Makes 2 servings

Favorite recipe from **National Fisheries
Institute**

TUNA CHOWDER FOR ONE

If you like, vary the vegetables by using mixed vegetable combinations packaged for single servings.

- **2 tablespoons chopped green onion**
- **½ cup diced mixed vegetables**
- **1 tablespoon vegetable oil**
- **1 tablespoon all-purpose flour**
- **1¼ cups low-fat milk**
- **½ teaspoon fines herbes or dried basil, crushed**
- **⅛ teaspoon paprika**
- **1 can (3¼ ounces) STARKIST® Tuna, drained and flaked**
- **Salt and pepper, to taste**

In a 2-quart saucepan, sauté onion and mixed vegetables in oil about 3 minutes or until vegetables are crisp-tender. Stir in flour until blended. Add milk all at once. Add fines herbes and paprika; cook and stir until mixture thickens and bubbles. Reduce heat; stir in tuna. Cook for 2 minutes more to heat through. Season with salt and pepper.

Makes 1 serving

Prep time: 15 minutes

RAINBOW TROUT PARMESAN

- **¼ cup seasoned bread crumbs**
- **4 teaspoons chopped parsley**
- **¼ cup fresh or dried grated Parmesan cheese**
- **1 tablespoon margarine, melted**
- **4 CLEAR SPRINGS® Brand Idaho Rainbow Trout fillets (4 ounces each)**

Combine bread crumbs with next 3 ingredients. Arrange trout, skin side down, in microwavable dish. Spread ¼ of bread crumb mixture evenly over each fillet; cover tightly. Microwave on HIGH 2 minutes. Rotate dish; microwave 2 to 4 minutes or until fish flakes with a fork. Remove from oven; garnish with tomatoes, if desired.

Makes 2 generous servings

Rainbow Trout Parmesan

SWORDFISH STEAKS WITH DILL-MUSTARD SAUCE

- **⅓ cup WISH-BONE® Italian Dressing**
- **2 swordfish or shark steaks, 1 inch thick (about 1 pound)**
- **½ cup dry white wine**
- **1 tablespoon Dijon-style mustard**
- **1 tablespoon snipped fresh dill**
- **⅛ teaspoon pepper**
- **½ cup whipping or heavy cream**

In large skillet, heat Italian dressing and cook fish over medium heat, turning once, 8 minutes or until fish flakes easily when tested with fork. Remove to serving platter and keep warm. Into skillet, add wine, then mustard, dill and pepper. Bring to a boil, then simmer, stirring occasionally, 8 minutes. Stir in cream and heat 1 minute or until thickened. Serve over fish. Garnish, if desired, with baby vegetables.

Makes about 2 servings

Substitution: Use 1 teaspoon dried dill weed for 1 tablespoon fresh dill.

SALMON WITH CHIVE SAUCE

- **½ cup MIRACLE WHIP® Salad Dressing**
- **¼ cup finely chopped fresh chives**
- **2 tablespoons finely chopped fresh thyme leaves or 2 teaspoons dried thyme leaves, crushed**
- **2 tablespoons finely chopped fresh dill or 2 teaspoons dried dill weed**
- **¼ teaspoon salt**
- **⅛ teaspoon pepper**
- **¼ cup dry white wine or chicken broth**
- **2 salmon steaks (approximately ¾ pound)**

- Mix together salad dressing, herbs, salt and pepper until well blended. Reserve ½ cup salad dressing mixture to serve later with cooked salmon. Stir wine into remaining salad dressing mixture; brush on salmon.

- Place salmon on grill over hot coals (coals will be glowing) or rack of broiler pan. Grill, covered, or broil 5 to 8 minutes on each side or until fish flakes easily with fork. Serve with reserved salad dressing mixture.

Makes 2 servings

Prep time: 10 minutes
Grill time: 16 minutes

Swordfish Steak with Dill-Mustard Sauce

MICROWAVED TROUT AMANDINE

2 trout fillets, about 6 ounces each
½ teaspoon lemon pepper
1 tablespoon margarine, divided
2 tablespoons sliced almonds
1 tablespoon lemon juice

Pat trout dry and sprinkle with lemon pepper. Place 1 teaspoon margarine in 9-inch glass pie plate. Microwave, uncovered, at HIGH 45 seconds or until melted. Stir in almonds; toss to coat. Microwave at HIGH 3 minutes or until light golden brown, stirring once. Let stand 5 minutes; reserve.

Place remaining 2 teaspoons margarine in 12×8-inch microwave-safe dish. Microwave at HIGH 45 seconds to melt. Stir in lemon juice. Coat fish in mixture and arrange, skin side down, in dish. Tuck under thin edges to make an even thickness. Cover loosely with waxed paper. Microwave at HIGH 2½ minutes. Allow to stand, covered, for 2 minutes. (Fish should flake easily with fork.) Transfer fish to warm plates and sprinkle with toasted almonds. Serve immediately.

Makes 2 servings

Favorite recipe from **National Fisheries Institute**

Microwaved Trout Amandine

SHRIMP DIANE

1¾ **pounds medium shrimp with heads and shells***
6 **tablespoons shrimp stock, divided**
⅜ **pound (1½ sticks) unsalted butter, divided**
¼ **cup very finely chopped green onions**
½ **teaspoon minced garlic**
2¼ **teaspoons Chef Paul Prudhomme's SEAFOOD MAGIC®**
½ **pound mushrooms, sliced into ¼-inch-thick pieces**
3 **tablespoons very finely chopped parsley leaves**
French bread, pasta or hot cooked rice

Rinse and peel the shrimp; refrigerate until needed. Use shells and heads to make shrimp stock.

In a large skillet, melt 1 stick of the butter over high heat. When almost melted, add the green onions, garlic and the Seafood Magic; stir well. Add the shrimp and sauté just until they turn pink, about 1 minute, carefully shaking the pan (versus stirring) in a back-and-forth motion.**

Add the mushrooms and 4 tablespoons of the stock, then add the remaining ½ stick butter in chunks and continue to shake the pan. Before the butter chunks are completely melted, add the parsley, then the remaining 2 tablespoons stock; continue cooking and shaking the pan until all ingredients are mixed thoroughly and butter sauce is the consistency of cream.

Serve immediately in a bowl with lots of French bread on the side, or serve over pasta or rice.

Makes 2 servings

*If shrimp with heads are not available, buy 1 pound of shrimp without heads (with shells, if possible, for making stock).

**A certain percentage of oil is released when butter is melted. Shaking the pan in a back-and-forth motion and the addition of stock to the melting butter keep the sauce from separating and having an oily texture; stirring doesn't produce the same effect.

SEDUCTIVE SHRIMP & CRAB

½ **pound crab or lobster meat**
¼ **pound peeled and deveined medium shrimp**
¾ **cup sour cream**
1 **teaspoon chopped fresh dill, tarragon *or* parsley**
Dash of salt
¼ **teaspoon TABASCO® pepper sauce**

Arrange the seafood in a shallow buttered casserole. Mix together remaining ingredients; pour over the seafood. Bake at 375°F for 10 minutes. For a crusty top, you may sprinkle the casserole with grated cheese or buttered bread crumbs before baking.

Makes 2 servings

PLEASING PLANNED OVERS

Maximize your time in the kitchen with this creative selection geared toward the time-conscious cook. These recipes are designed to create "leftovers," allowing you to stretch each and every one into an exciting new meal idea.

CHEESE-TURKEY CRÊPES

2 frozen Basic Crêpes (see page 72)
½ cup frozen whole green beans
4 slices (1 ounce each) Muenster cheese, cut in half
2 slices (1 ounce each) deli-style turkey breast, each cut into 4 pieces
½ can (16 ounces) whole berry cranberry sauce

Thaw crêpes as directed in Basic Crêpes recipe. Preheat oven to 350°F. Cook green beans according to package directions; drain. To assemble, place half the cheese down center of each crêpe (pale side up). Top with turkey and beans. Fold opposite edges to overlap filling. Place, seam side down, in buttered 8-inch square baking dish. Bake 15 to 18 minutes or until cheese is melted. Meanwhile, heat cranberry sauce in small saucepan over low heat, stirring frequently. To serve, spoon sauce over each crêpe. Serve immediately.

Makes 2 servings

Notes:
Place remaining ½ can cranberry sauce in covered plastic container. Store in refrigerator for use later in the week.

Leftover or deli slices of ham or chicken breast may be substituted for turkey. No other changes need be made since green beans and Muenster cheese harmonize with any of the meats.

Favorite recipe from **American Dairy Association**

Top to bottom: Cheesy Vegetable Crêpes (page 72); Cheese-Turkey Crêpes

CHEESY VEGETABLE CRÊPES

2 frozen Basic Crêpes
1 package (10 ounces) frozen ratatouille
½ cup (2 ounces) shredded Cheddar cheese

Thaw crêpes as directed in Basic Crêpes recipe. Preheat oven to 350°F. Heat ratatouille according to package directions; drain, reserving liquid. To assemble, spoon half of ratatouille down center of each crêpe (pale side up). Sprinkle each with 2 tablespoons cheese. Fold opposite edges to overlap filling. Place, seam side down, in buttered baking dish. Sprinkle each with 2 tablespoons cheese. Bake 10 to 12 minutes or until cheese is melted. Meanwhile, heat reserved liquid until hot and bubbly, stirring occasionally. To serve, spoon sauce over each crêpe. Serve immediately.

Makes 2 servings

Note: Creamed vegetables may be substituted for ratatouille. In the interest of economy, the vegetables may be leftover ones that you cream for this purpose.

Favorite recipe from **American Dairy Association**

BASIC CRÊPES

1 cup all-purpose flour
1½ cups milk
2 eggs
1 tablespoon butter, melted
¼ teaspoon salt
Butter

Combine first 5 ingredients in small mixing bowl; beat with rotary beater or wire whisk until blended. Heat a lightly buttered 6-inch skillet or crêpe pan. Remove from heat; spoon in about 2 tablespoons batter. Lift and tilt skillet to spread batter evenly. Return to heat; brown on one side only. To remove, invert pan over paper toweling; remove crêpe. Repeat with remaining batter, buttering skillet as needed. To freeze, layer crêpes between 2 sheets of waxed paper. Overwrap with aluminum foil; freeze. Crêpes can be kept frozen 2 to 4 months. To defrost, remove only number needed. Keep crêpes covered with waxed paper; let thaw at room temperature about 1 hour. Frozen crêpes make interesting meals at a later date.

Makes 16 to 18 crêpes

Favorite recipe from **American Dairy Association**

Herb-Seasoned Steak with Savory Squash

HERB-SEASONED STEAK WITH SAVORY SQUASH

1 beef top round steak, cut 1 inch thick (approximately 1 pound)
1 cup cubed butternut squash (½-inch pieces)
1 small onion, thinly sliced
½ cup apple juice
¼ teaspoon salt
2 cloves garlic, minced
1 teaspoon *each:* **dried basil, thyme leaves**
½ teaspoon cracked black pepper
1 teaspoon olive oil
1 tablespoon butter or margarine

Combine squash, onion, apple juice and salt in medium frying pan. Simmer, covered, 20 minutes or until tender. Meanwhile, combine garlic, basil, thyme, pepper and oil to form thick paste. Spread herb paste evenly over both sides of beef top round steak. Heat large nonstick frying pan over medium-high heat. Add steak and cook 13 to 16 minutes to doneness desired (rare to medium), turning once. Uncover squash and cook 5 minutes or until liquid is evaporated. Remove from heat; stir in butter. Carve half the steak* into thin slices. Serve steak with squash.

Makes 2 servings

Prep time: 15 minutes
Cook time: 25 minutes

*Reserve remaining steak for Saucy Steak and Pasta (see page 75).

Favorite recipe from **National Live Stock and Meat Board**

TURKEY WITH WILD RICE

**1 package (about 2 pounds)
LOUIS RICH® Fresh Turkey
Breast Portion
1 box (6¾ ounces) instant long
grain and wild rice mix
2 tablespoons slivered almonds
1 box (10 ounces) frozen
chopped broccoli, thawed**

Rinse turkey. Combine rice seasoning mix, almonds and 1 cup water in 3-quart casserole. Add turkey. Bake in 325°F oven 1 hour. Stir in 2¼ cups hot water, rice and broccoli. Bake 30 minutes to an internal temperature of 170°F. Let stand 10 minutes before slicing. Wrap and refrigerate any remaining turkey and rice. To reheat, place 3 slices turkey and about 1 cup rice mixture on plate. Cover with plastic wrap, turning back corner to vent. Microwave at HIGH 2 to 3 minutes, stirring rice halfway through heating.

Makes 4 servings

MICROWAVE: Rinse turkey. Combine rice seasoning mix, almonds and ¾ cup water in 3-quart glass casserole. Add turkey, skin side down. Cover with plastic wrap, turning back corner to vent. Microwave at HIGH 11 minutes per pound or until internal temperature reaches 170°F, turning turkey over halfway through cooking. Place turkey on platter; keep warm. Add rice, 1¾ cups hot water and broccoli to casserole; cover. Microwave at HIGH 5 minutes. Let stand 5 minutes.

Turkey with Wild Rice

SAUCY STEAK AND PASTA

6 ounces cooked beef top round steak*
1 can (16 ounces) whole tomatoes, broken up
2 tablespoons chopped parsley
Dash of crushed red pepper
2 tablespoons grated Parmesan cheese, divided
1 cup cooked rotelle or spiral-shaped pasta

Carve beef top round steak into thin slices; reserve. Combine tomatoes, parsley and red pepper in medium saucepan. Bring to a boil; simmer, uncovered, over medium heat 12 to 15 minutes. Stir in 1 tablespoon cheese. Place an equal amount of pasta on two dinner plates; spoon sauce over pasta. Arrange beef slices over sauce; sprinkle with remaining cheese.

Makes 2 servings

Prep time: 10 minutes
Cook time: 12 to 15 minutes

*Use reserved cooked beef top round steak from Herb-Seasoned Steak with Savory Squash (see page 73).

Favorite recipe from **National Live Stock and Meat Board**

BRAN MUFFINS

1 cup boiling water
3 cups bran cereal
½ cup (1 stick) butter, softened
¾ cup sugar
2 eggs
2 cups buttermilk
2½ cups all-purpose flour
2½ teaspoons baking soda
1½ teaspoons salt

Combine boiling water and 1 cup bran cereal; let stand, uncovered, 5 minutes. Cream butter and sugar in a large mixing bowl until light and fluffy. Beat in eggs. Stir in bran-water mixture and buttermilk. Combine dry ingredients. Gradually add to batter. Stir in remaining 2 cups bran cereal. Store batter in covered container in refrigerator up to 1 month. To bake, fill buttered muffin cups ⅔ full. Bake in preheated 400°F oven 20 to 22 minutes. Serve warm with butter. (Bake only as many as needed; keep remaining batter refrigerated for convenience.)

Makes 2 dozen muffins

Variation: Sprinkle 1 tablespoon of any of the following in each buttered muffin cup: chopped dates, raisins or chopped nuts. Bake as directed above.

Favorite recipe from **American Dairy Association**

ROUND STEAK FOR FOUR DIFFERENT MEALS

To provide four meals, divide one beef round steak, cut 1 inch thick (2½ to 3 pounds), by cutting along natural seams to divide into top round, bottom round and eye muscles. Cut bone free from steak, including small portions of top and bottom round around bone.

EASY BEEF AND BROCCOLI STIR-FRY

  1 **beef top round steak, cut 1 inch thick (about 1½ pounds)**
  3 **tablespoons** *each:* **soy sauce, dry sherry**
  1 **tablespoon sesame oil**
  2 **teaspoons sugar**
  1 **large clove garlic, minced**
  ⅛ **teaspoon crushed red pepper**
  2 **tablespoons vegetable oil**
  3 **cups broccoli flowerets, blanched**
  1 **teaspoon cornstarch**
  ¼ **cup unsalted peanuts**
    Sliced green onions

Cut beef top round steak in half; wrap and freeze remaining steak for another meal.* Partially freeze half of steak to firm; slice diagonally across the grain into strips ⅛ inch thick. Combine soy sauce, sherry, sesame oil, sugar, garlic and red pepper. Place beef strips in plastic bag or utility dish. Pour marinade over beef strips, stirring to coat. Close bag securely or cover dish and marinate in refrigerator 30 minutes. Drain beef

*Freeze remaining steak for Quick Beef Sauté (recipe follows).

strips; reserve marinade. Stir-fry beef in hot vegetable oil in wok or large frying pan 2 minutes; add broccoli and continue cooking 2 minutes. Combine cornstarch and reserved marinade; add to beef mixture and cook, stirring until sauce thickens. Sprinkle peanuts and green onions over stir-fry.

Makes 2 to 3 servings

Freezing time: 30 minutes
Prep time: 15 minutes
Marinating time: 30 minutes
Cook time: 7 to 8 minutes

QUICK BEEF SAUTÉ

 12 **ounces beef top round steak, cut 1 inch thick**
  ¼ **cup dairy sour cream**
  3 **tablespoons prepared horseradish, divided**
  ½ **cup red wine**
  1 **teaspoon dry mustard**
  ¼ **teaspoon freshly ground black pepper**
    Oil
  ⅛ **teaspoon salt, divided**

Combine sour cream and 1 tablespoon horseradish; cover and refrigerate. Combine wine, remaining 2 tablespoons horseradish and mustard. Place steak in plastic bag; pour marinade over steak, turning to coat. Close bag securely and marinate in refrigerator 6 to 8 hours (or overnight, if desired), turning once. Remove steak from marinade; pat dry with paper towels. Press pepper into steak. Heat heavy frying pan over medium to medium-high heat; brush lightly with oil. Add steak and panbroil 4 to 5 minutes; turn. Sprinkle with salt and brown on second side, 4 to 5 minutes, cooking to rare or medium-rare. Sprinkle salt on second side. Slice thinly across the grain and serve with horseradish sauce.

Makes 2 to 3 servings

Prep time: 10 minutes
Marinating time: 6 to 8 hours
Cook time: 8 to 10 minutes

BEEF RAGOUT

- **1 beef bottom round steak, cut 1 inch thick, plus bone (about 1 pound)**
- **1 teaspoon dried thyme leaves**
- **½ teaspoon salt**
- **¼ teaspoon pepper**
- **2 tablespoons oil**
- **1 large onion, cut into wedges**
- **2 cloves garlic, minced**
- **1 can (13¾ ounces) single-strength beef broth**
- **½ cup dry red wine**
- **4 medium carrots, thinly sliced**
- **2 cups sliced mushrooms**
- **Cooked noodles**

Cut beef into 1-inch pieces; cut each in half. Combine thyme, salt and pepper; sprinkle evenly over beef. Brown beef in oil in large frying pan over medium-high heat. Stir in onion and garlic and continue cooking 1 to 2 minutes. Add broth, wine and the bone. Reduce heat. Cover tightly and simmer 1¼ hours. Stir in carrots and mushrooms. Continue cooking, uncovered, 40 to 45 minutes, or until carrots are tender and sauce slightly thickens. Discard bone; remove marrow from bone and stir into sauce, if desired. Serve over cooked noodles.

Makes 2 to 3 servings

Prep time: 20 minutes
Cook time: 2 hours

Favorite recipe from **National Live Stock and Meat Board**

(continued)

Clockwise from top left: Quick Beef Sauté; Easy Beef and Broccoli Stir-Fry; Tangy Eye Round Steak (page 78); Beef Ragout

TANGY EYE ROUND STEAK

**1 beef eye round steak, cut
1 inch thick
Juice of 1 lime
½ teaspoon _each_: garlic salt,
ground coriander, cumin
¼ teaspoon freshly ground black
pepper
Oil**

Combine lime juice, garlic salt, coriander, cumin and pepper. Place steak in plastic bag or utility dish; pour marinade over steak, turning to coat. Close bag securely or cover dish and marinate in refrigerator 30 minutes, turning once. Remove steak from marinade. Heat small frying pan over medium heat. Brush pan lightly with oil. Add steak and panbroil 8 minutes, turning once. Carve across the grain into thin slices.

Makes 2 servings

Prep time: 5 minutes
Marinating time: 30 minutes
Cook time: 8 minutes

Favorite recipe from **National Live Stock and Meat Board**

SWISS IRISH PANCAKES

**4 medium-size boiling potatoes
(about 1¼ pounds), peeled,
shredded and well drained
1 cup (4 ounces) shredded
Swiss cheese
¼ cup grated onion
3 eggs
¼ cup all-purpose flour
¼ teaspoon _each_: salt, pepper
Applesauce
Vegetable oil**

Combine potatoes, cheese, onion, eggs, flour, salt and pepper; mix until well blended. Heat enough oil to just cover bottom of a large heavy skillet. (You may have to add more oil as you continue to fry pancakes.) Drop ¼ cup batter into hot oil to form a 4-inch pancake. Cook over medium-high heat until golden and crisp on both sides. Drain on paper toweling. Serve immediately with chilled applesauce.

Makes 12 (4-inch) pancakes

FREEZING INSTRUCTIONS:
Pancakes can be frozen. To reheat, place frozen pancakes on baking sheet in preheated 350°F oven. Heat 12 to 15 minutes. Serve immediately. DO NOT microwave.

Favorite recipe from **American Dairy Association**

BASIC BEEF MIXTURE

**2 pounds ground round steak
⅔ cup chopped onion
½ cup chopped celery
2 packages (0.75 ounce each)
mushroom gravy mix
1½ cups water
1 tablespoon _each_: beef
bouillon, Worcestershire
sauce**

Cook ground round, onion and celery until beef is brown and crumbly. Drain off excess fat. Stir in remaining ingredients. Simmer, uncovered, 5 minutes, stirring frequently. Place 1¾ cups beef mixture in each of 3 (1-pint) containers. Freeze until ready to use (up to 3 months). Thaw in refrigerator 24 to 48 hours.

Makes 5¼ cups

BEEF STROGANOFF

1 package Basic Beef Mixture, thawed (see page 78)
1 jar (2½ ounces) sliced mushrooms, drained
⅛ teaspoon garlic powder
½ cup dairy sour cream
1 tablespoon flour
Hot buttered noodles
Parsley, if desired

Combine beef mixture, mushrooms and garlic powder. Simmer, uncovered, 5 minutes. Combine sour cream and flour until well blended. Stir into beef mixture. Reduce heat to low. Heat through, but do not boil. Serve over hot buttered noodles garnished with parsley.

Makes 2 servings

PEPPERED BEEF

1 package Basic Beef Mixture, thawed (see page 78)
½ medium green pepper, cut into julienne strips
½ cup *each*: chopped tomato, plain yogurt, tomato sauce
⅛ teaspoon garlic powder
Hot buttered rice

Combine beef mixture, green pepper and tomato. Bring to boiling; simmer, covered, 10 minutes. Meanwhile, combine yogurt, tomato sauce and garlic powder. Remove meat mixture from heat. Stir in yogurt mixture. Heat over low heat until heated through. Do not boil. Serve over hot buttered rice.

Makes 2 servings

Favorite recipe from **American Dairy Association**

MINI-LOAVES OLÉ

1 package (1 pound) LOUIS RICH® Ground Turkey, thawed
1 can (15 ounces) tomato sauce
⅓ cup crushed tortilla chips
¼ cup chopped onion
2 tablespoons chopped green pepper
1 package (1¼ ounces) taco seasoning mix

Combine ingredients, reserving 1 cup tomato sauce. Spoon into 6 (6-ounce) custard cups. Place in shallow baking pan. Bake in 350°F oven 25 minutes or until no longer pink in center. Heat reserved tomato sauce and serve with mini-loaves. Remove remaining mini-loaves from custard cups; cool. Wrap and refrigerate. Crumble, heat and use to fill taco shells or top mixed greens for taco salad. Or, wrap and freeze for up to 3 months. To reheat, place 2 frozen mini-loaves on plate. Cover with waxed paper. Microwave at HIGH 5 minutes, rotating plate halfway through cooking. Let stand, covered, 3 minutes.

Makes 6 servings

MICROWAVE: Combine ingredients as directed above. Spoon into 6 custard cups. Place on plate. Cover with waxed paper. Microwave at HIGH 8 to 10 minutes or until no longer pink in center, rotating plate halfway through cooking.

Turkey Cordon Bleu

TURKEY CORDON BLEU

1 package (about 1 pound)
LOUIS RICH® Fresh Turkey
Breast Tenderloin Steaks
1½ cups seasoned croutons,
crushed
¼ teaspoon paprika
¼ cup butter, melted
2 slices (1 ounce each)
LOUIS RICH® Turkey Ham
2 slices (1 ounce each) Swiss
cheese
4 teaspoons Dijon mustard

Pound turkey between pieces of plastic wrap to uniform thickness. Combine crouton crumbs and paprika in shallow dish. Dip turkey into melted butter, then into crumb mixture. Place ½ slice turkey ham and ½ slice cheese on each turkey steak; spread each with 1 teaspoon mustard. Roll up and secure with toothpicks. Arrange in shallow baking dish. Bake 2 in 400°F oven 30 minutes or until no longer pink in center. Remove toothpicks before serving. Wrap 2 and freeze for up to 3 months. To cook frozen, bake in 400°F oven 45 minutes.

Makes 4 servings

MICROWAVE: To melt butter, place butter in glass baking dish. Microwave at HIGH 45 to 60 seconds. Prepare turkey and assemble as directed. Arrange in circle in glass baking dish. Cover with waxed paper. Microwave at HIGH 5 minutes. Rearrange uncooked portions toward outer edge of dish. Microwave at HIGH 5 to 7 minutes more or until no longer pink in center.

FREEZE 'N BAKE TURKEY CUTLETS OR SLICES

Produce tender, juicy turkey cutlets or slices anytime. Simply follow the recipe and keep these pre-breaded, frozen cutlets or slices on hand. Creative entrées can be made in a flash.

1 egg white
1 tablespoon water
½ cup seasoned bread crumbs
1 pound Turkey Breast Cutlets or
Slices, ⅛ to ⅜ inch thick

1. In shallow bowl, beat egg white and water together. Set aside.

2. Spread bread crumbs over shallow plate.

3. Dip turkey into egg mixture, then into crumbs.

4. Arrange breaded turkey slices on a cookie sheet. Freeze 30 to 45 minutes. Transfer frozen turkey slices to self-closing freezer bag and return to freezer until ready to bake.

5. When ready to prepare, preheat oven to 400°F.

6. Spray cookie sheet with non-stick cooking oil. Arrange frozen cutlets or slices on sheet; bake approximately 9 minutes for 1/8-inch slices and 13 minutes for 3/8-inch slices or until slices are no longer pink in center.

Try one of the sauces below for tasty toppers or make up your own.

Spicy Orange Sauce: In a small saucepan over medium-high heat, melt 1/4 cup orange marmalade. Stir in 3/4 to 1 teaspoon prepared horseradish; heat until warm. Serve sauce over 2 cooked turkey cutlets or slices.

Toasted Almond Sauce: In a small nonstick skillet over medium heat, toast 1 1/2 teaspoons slivered almonds until browned. Remove skillet from heat and wait 45 seconds. Quickly stir in 1/4 cup peach yogurt and 1/2 teaspoon curry. Serve sauce over 2 cooked cutlet slices.

Turkey Parmigiana In-a-Hurry: Prepare Freeze 'n Bake Turkey Cutlets or Slices according to directions, baking 6 minutes for 1/8-inch slices and 10 minutes for 3/8-inch slices. Top with 1/2 cup spaghetti sauce and 2 slices (1 ounce each) mozzarella cheese. Return to oven and continue baking approximately 5 minutes or until cutlets are no longer pink in center, sauce bubbles and cheese melts. Serve over cooked spaghetti, if desired.

Favorite recipe from **National Turkey Federation**

INDIVIDUAL SOUFFLÉS

1/4 **cup (1/2 stick) butter**
1/4 **cup all-purpose flour**
1/4 **teaspoon salt**
  Dash cayenne pepper
  1 **cup** *each:* **milk, shredded Cheddar cheese (4 ounces)**
1/4 **cup grated Parmesan cheese**
  6 **eggs, separated**
1/4 **teaspoon cream of tartar**

Melt butter over low heat. Stir in flour, salt and cayenne. Cook until smooth, stirring constantly. Remove from heat. Gradually stir in milk. Bring to a boil over medium heat, stirring constantly. Boil and stir 1 minute. Remove from heat and stir in cheeses until melted. If necessary, return to low heat to finish melting cheeses. (Do not boil.) Blend a little hot mixture into slightly beaten egg yolks; return all to saucepan and blend thoroughly. Beat egg whites with cream of tartar until stiff, but not dry. Fold cheese sauce into egg whites. Turn mixture into 5 individual soufflé dishes, filling 3/4 full. For immediate service, bake one or more soufflés in preheated 300°F oven 30 minutes. Serve immediately. Carefully wrap remaining unbaked soufflés in freezer wrap and freeze up to 1 month. To bake frozen soufflé, unwrap and place directly from freezer into preheated 300°F oven for about 1 hour and 10 minutes.

Makes 5 servings

Favorite recipe from **American Dairy Association**

DAZZLING DESSERTS & DRINKS

No meal is complete without the luscious flavor of a delectable dessert. Discover pure dessert satisfaction with this sensational collection of melt-in-the-mouth treats, just perfect for the smaller household.

PRALINE BROWNIES

BROWNIES
- 1 package DUNCAN HINES® Brownies Plus Milk Chocolate Chunks Mix
- 2 eggs
- ⅓ cup water
- ⅓ cup CRISCO® Oil or CRISCO® PURITAN® Oil
- ¾ cup chopped pecans

TOPPING
- ¾ cup firmly packed brown sugar
- ¾ cup chopped pecans
- ¼ cup butter or margarine, melted
- 2 tablespoons milk
- ½ teaspoon vanilla extract

1. Preheat oven to 350°F. Grease 9-inch square pan.

2. **For brownies,** combine brownie mix, eggs, water, oil and ¾ cup pecans in large bowl. Stir with spoon until well blended, about 50 strokes. Spread in pan. Bake at 350°F for 35 to 40 minutes. Remove from oven.

3. **For topping,** combine brown sugar, ¾ cup pecans, melted butter, milk and vanilla extract in small bowl. Stir with spoon until well blended. Spread over hot brownies. Return to oven. Bake for 15 minutes or until topping is set. Cool completely. Cut into bars.

Makes 16 brownies

Tip: To keep leftover pecans fresh, store in freezer in airtight container.

FREEZING INSTRUCTIONS: Wrap each bar in square of plastic wrap or waxed paper. Place wrapped brownies in plastic resealable freezer bag and freeze for up to 6 months.

Praline Brownies

KAHLÚA® Tiramisu for Two

KAHLÚA® TIRAMISU FOR TWO

12 small packaged ladyfingers
2 egg yolks*
½ cup powdered sugar
4 ounces softened cream cheese, beaten until fluffy
⅓ cup whipping cream, whipped
½ teaspoon instant espresso powder
1 tablespoon water
¼ cup KAHLÚA®
1 ounce semisweet chocolate, chopped fine
2 teaspoons unsweetened cocoa powder

Arrange ladyfingers in single layer on baking sheet. Toast at 325°F for 10 minutes. Set aside. In bowl, whisk yolks with sugar until smooth and thick. Whisk in cream cheese. Fold in whipped cream.

In separate bowl, dissolve espresso powder in water. Stir in KAHLÚA®. In third bowl, combine chopped chocolate and cocoa.

Place 2 tablespoons cream cheese mixture in bottom of each of two (12-ounce) wine goblets or dessert dishes. Top each with three ladyfingers, 3 to 4 teaspoons KAHLÚA® mixture and ⅓ cup cream cheese mixture. Cover each with ¼ of the chocolate mixture, three ladyfingers and 3 to 4 teaspoons KAHLÚA® mixture. Top each dessert with ½ of the remaining cream cheese mixture; smooth top. Sprinkle with remaining chocolate mixture. Cover and chill several hours or overnight before serving.

Makes 2 servings

Variation: For KAHLÚA® Banana-Almond Tiramisu, add 1 medium banana, sliced ¼ inch thick (about twenty slices), and 4 teaspoons toasted slivered or chopped almonds. Layer five banana slices over each layer of ladyfingers and sprinkle 1 teaspoon almonds over second and third layers of cream cheese.

*Use clean, uncracked eggs.

24-HOUR JUICE SENSATION

Fresh mint sprigs
¾ cup DOLE® Pine-Orange-Banana Juice
½ cup diet lemon-lime soda *or* mineral water, chilled
Lime slices

• Rub tall glass with mint. Drop mint in glass.

• Pour in juice and soda. Add lime.
Makes 1 serving

STRAWBERRY-BANANA SHAKE

**1 cup fresh strawberries,
    washed and hulled**
1 small banana, cut into chunks
1 cup plain nonfat yogurt
2 tablespoons sugar
½ teaspoon vanilla extract
6 ice cubes

In a blender or food processor,
combine all ingredients. Process
until smooth.

Makes 2 (8-ounce) servings

Favorite recipe from **The Sugar
Association, Inc.**

QUICK APPLE TART

**2 teaspoons reduced-calorie
    cream cheese, softened**
**1 (5½×2½-inch) HONEY MAID®
    Grahams**
1 tablespoon apple pie filling

Spread cream cheese on cracker;
top with apple pie filling. Place on
small microwavable plate.
Microwave at HIGH (100% power)
for 10 to 15 seconds or until warm.
Serve immediately.

Makes 1 serving

YOGURT AND APPLE DESSERT

**1 cup DANNON® Plain or Vanilla
    Yogurt**
**1 cup DANNON® Dutch Apple
    Yogurt**
½ cup slivered toasted almonds
**½ cup raisins
    Maple syrup *or* sugar, to taste
    Nutmeg, if desired**

Combine all ingredients; chill.
Serve in parfait glasses.

Makes 2 generous servings

Note: Dessert is better if raisins
are mixed in with the yogurt the
day before.

SWEET CHERRIES ROMANOFF-STYLE

**1 cup halved and pitted
    Northwest fresh sweet
    cherries**
**1 tablespoon *each*: orange-
    flavored liqueur, black
    currant liqueur**
1 teaspoon sugar
**2 tablespoons dairy sour cream
    Toasted sliced almonds**

Combine cherries with liqueurs
and sugar; refrigerate several
hours. Spoon cherries into 2
individual dessert dishes. Gently
stir 2 teaspoons liqueur from
cherries into sour cream; spoon
over cherries. Garnish with
almonds.

Makes 2 servings

Favorite recipe from **Northwest Cherry
Growers**

Sweet Cherries Romanoff-Style

JUMBO CHUNKY COOKIES

1 cup (2 sticks) margarine or
    butter, softened
¾ cup firmly packed brown sugar
¾ cup granulated sugar
2 eggs
1 teaspoon vanilla
1¾ cups all-purpose flour
½ cup quick oats
1 teaspoon baking soda
½ teaspoon cinnamon
¼ teaspoon salt
1 package (8 ounces) BAKER'S®
    Semi-Sweet Chocolate, cut
    into chunks, *or* 1 package
    (12 ounces) BAKER'S®
    Semi-Sweet Real Chocolate
    Chips
1 cup BAKER'S® ANGEL
    FLAKE® Coconut
⅔ cup chopped nuts
½ cup raisins (optional)

HEAT oven to 375°F.

BEAT margarine, sugars, eggs and
vanilla until light and fluffy. Mix in
flour, oats, baking soda, cinnamon
and salt.

STIR in chocolate, coconut, nuts
and raisins. Drop by rounded
tablespoonfuls, 2½ inches apart,
onto ungreased cookie sheets.

BAKE for 15 minutes or until
golden brown. Remove from
cookie sheets to cool on wire
racks.

Makes about 2½ dozen cookies

Prep time: 20 minutes
Baking time: 15 minutes

FREEZING INSTRUCTIONS: Store
completely cooled cookies in
freezer-weight wrap or in an
airtight container with waxed paper
or plastic wrap between layers.
Freeze for up to three months.

PEANUT BUTTER SAUCE

½ cup super chunk peanut butter
½ cup light or dark corn syrup
2 tablespoons milk

In small bowl, stir peanut butter,
corn syrup and milk until well
blended. Serve over ice cream.
Store in tightly covered container in
refrigerator.

Makes 1 cup

Chocolate-Peanut Butter Sauce:
Follow recipe for Peanut Butter
Sauce. Omit milk. Add ½ cup
chocolate-flavored syrup. Makes
1½ cups

**Chocolate Chip-Peanut Butter
Sauce:** Follow recipe for Peanut
Butter Sauce. Add ½ cup miniature
semisweet chocolate pieces.
Makes 1⅓ cups

**Fruit and Honey-Peanut Butter
Sauce:** Follow recipe for Peanut
Butter Sauce. Reduce corn syrup
to ¼ cup. Add ½ cup coarsely
chopped apple or banana, ¼ cup
honey and ⅛ teaspoon ground
cinnamon. Makes 1½ cups

Peanut Butter and Jelly Sauce:
Follow recipe for Peanut Butter
Sauce. Omit milk. Add ½ cup
grape or strawberry jelly, melted.
Makes about 1⅓ cups

Mocha-Peanut Butter Sauce:
Follow recipe for Peanut Butter
Sauce. Omit corn syrup and milk.
Add ¾ cup chocolate-flavored
syrup and ¼ cup strong coffee.
Makes 1⅓ cups

Favorite recipe from **Oklahoma Peanut
Commission**

ONE BOWL® Brownies

ONE BOWL® BROWNIES

4 squares BAKER'S® Unsweetened Chocolate
¾ cup (1½ sticks) margarine or butter
2 cups sugar
3 eggs
1 teaspoon vanilla
1 cup all-purpose flour
1 cup chopped nuts (optional)

HEAT oven to 350°F.

MICROWAVE chocolate and margarine in large microwavable bowl on HIGH 2 minutes or until margarine is melted. **Stir until chocolate is completely melted.**

STIR sugar into melted chocolate mixture. Mix in eggs and vanilla until well blended. Stir in flour and nuts. Spread in greased 13×9-inch pan.

BAKE for 30 to 35 minutes or until toothpick inserted into center comes out with fudgy crumbs. **Do not overbake.** Cool in pan; cut into squares.

Makes about 24 brownies

Prep time: 10 minutes
Baking time: 30 to 35 minutes

Tips:
• For cakelike brownies, stir in ½ cup milk with eggs and vanilla. Increase flour to 1½ cups.

• When using a glass baking dish, reduce oven temperature to 325°F.

FREEZING INSTRUCTIONS: Store completely cooled brownies in freezer-weight wrap or in an airtight container and freeze for up to three months.

Miniature Cheesecakes

MINIATURE CHEESECAKES

CRUST
- ⅔ **cup graham cracker crumbs**
- 2 **tablespoons sugar**
- 2 **tablespoons PARKAY®**
  Margarine, melted

FILLING
- 2 **packages (8 ounces each)**
  PHILADELPHIA BRAND®
  Cream Cheese, softened
- ½ **cup sugar**
- 1 **tablespoon lemon juice**
- 1 **teaspoon grated lemon peel**
- ½ **teaspoon vanilla**
- 2 **eggs**
  KRAFT® Strawberry,
  Raspberry or Apricot
  Preserves

- **Crust:** Heat oven to 325°F.

- Mix crumbs, sugar and margarine. Press rounded measuring tablespoonful of crumb mixture onto bottom of each of 12 paper-lined muffin cups. Bake 5 minutes.

- **Filling:** Beat cream cheese, sugar, juice, peel and vanilla at medium speed with electric mixer until well blended. Add eggs, 1 at a time, mixing well after each addition. Pour over crusts, filling each cup ¾ full.

- Bake 25 minutes. Cool before removing from pan. Refrigerate. Top with preserves just before serving.

Makes 12 servings

Prep time: 20 minutes plus refrigerating
Cook time: 25 minutes

Variation: Substitute fresh fruit for KRAFT® Preserves.

FREEZING INSTRUCTIONS: Wrap chilled cheesecakes individually in plastic wrap; freeze. Let stand at room temperature 40 minutes before serving.

CHOCOLATE COEUR À LA CRÈME WITH STRAWBERRY SAUCE

½ **cup whipping cream, divided**
3 **tablespoons HERSHEY'S® Cocoa**
1 **tablespoon butter, softened**
1 **package (3 ounces) cream cheese, softened**
½ **cup powdered sugar**
½ **teaspoon vanilla extract Strawberry Sauce (recipe follows)**

Line two (½-cup) coeur à la crème molds or two (6-ounce) custard cups with double thickness of dampened cheese cloth, extending far enough beyond edges to enclose filling completely. In small saucepan, combine ¼ cup whipping cream, cocoa and butter; cook over low heat, stirring constantly, until smooth. Remove from heat; cool.

In small mixer bowl, beat cream cheese, powdered sugar and vanilla until smooth. Add cocoa mixture, blending well. Add remaining ¼ cup whipping cream; beat until well blended. Spoon mixture into prepared molds. Fold cheesecloth over top. Place molds on wire rack set in tray or deep plate. Refrigerate 8 hours or overnight. To serve, pull back cheesecloth and invert each mold onto a chilled dessert plate; carefully remove cheesecloth. Serve with Strawberry Sauce.

Makes 2 servings

Strawberry Sauce: In food processor bowl or blender container, purée 1 package (10 ounces) frozen strawberries in light syrup, thawed. Strain purée through fine sieve into small bowl. Stir in 1 tablespoon kirsch (cherry brandy), if desired. Makes about 1 cup

CHOCOLATE LOVER'S MOUSSE FOR TWO

2 **tablespoons sugar**
½ **teaspoon unflavored gelatin**
¼ **cup milk**
½ **cup HERSHEY'S® MINI CHIPS® Semi-Sweet Chocolate**
1 **tablespoon orange-flavored liqueur or rum *or* 1 teaspoon vanilla extract**
½ **cup cold whipping cream Additional whipping cream, whipped (optional)**

In small saucepan, stir together sugar and gelatin; stir in milk. Let stand 2 minutes to soften gelatin. Cook over medium heat, stirring constantly, until mixture just begins to boil. Remove from heat. Immediately add small chocolate chips; stir until melted. Stir in liqueur; cool to room temperature. In small mixer bowl, beat whipping cream until stiff; gradually add chocolate mixture, folding gently just until blended. Refrigerate. Garnish with additional whipped cream, if desired.

Makes 2 servings

FRESH YOGURT SUNDAE

- 1 cup DANNON® Plain Yogurt
- 2 tablespoons honey
- 2 tablespoons chopped almonds
- 2 or 3 chopped dates

Spoon yogurt into a chilled stem glass or bowl. Pour honey over yogurt; sprinkle with almonds and dates.

Makes 1 serving

HAWAIIAN SUNRISE

- ½ cup DOLE® Pineapple Juice
- 1 ounce tequila
- ½ ounce orange-flavored liqueur
- 1 lemon wedge, squeezed
  Crushed ice
- ¾ ounce grenadine

- Combine pineapple juice, tequila, liqueur, lemon juice and crushed ice to fill glass. Stir.

- Slowly pour in grenadine and allow to settle.

Makes 1 serving

Hawaiian Sunrise

APRICOT SMOOTHIE

Call it a shake, a health drink or a smoothie. Anyone who drinks it will call it delicious. Wheat germ adds a very appealing mild, nutty flavor.

- 1 cup drained canned apricot halves
- ½ pint apricot-pineapple or orange yogurt
- 1 cup milk
- 4 to 6 ice cubes
- 2 tablespoons wheat germ (optional)

Combine all ingredients in electric blender; blend until smooth and thick.

Makes 3 cups or 2 servings

Favorite recipe from **California Apricot Advisory Board**

KAHLÚA® WHITE CHOCOLATE FONDUE

- 2 cinnamon sticks
- ⅔ cup whipping cream
- 6 ounces white chocolate, chopped
- ¼ cup KAHLÚA®
  Bite-size pieces of fruit, such as strawberries, raspberries, bananas, pineapple chunks, apple or orange wedges, and cubes of pound cake *or* cookies

Cut cinnamon sticks in half lengthwise; break each half into several pieces.

In small saucepan, combine cream and half of cinnamon pieces. Bring to rolling boil; remove from heat. Cover and let stand 15 minutes. Add remaining cinnamon stick pieces; return to rolling boil. Remove from heat. Cover and let stand 15 minutes longer.

Place white chocolate in medium bowl. Return cream to boil once more; pour through strainer into bowl with white chocolate. Let stand 1 to 2 minutes; stir until smooth. Stir in KAHLÚA®. Serve warm in fondue pot (if desired) with bite-size pieces of fruit, cake or cookies.

Makes 2 cups

Note: Fondue can stand at room temperature for several hours or in refrigerator several days. Before serving, reheat until warm. Fruit should be patted dry to allow fondue to adhere to surface.

SPECIAL BANANAS FOSTER

2 firm, small DOLE® Bananas, peeled
1 tablespoon lemon juice
¼ cup brown sugar, packed
2 tablespoons margarine
 Dash of ground cinnamon
3 tablespoons light rum
 Vanilla or coffee ice cream

Cut bananas in half lengthwise, then crosswise into quarters. Drizzle with lemon juice. Heat brown sugar and margarine together in a 10-inch skillet until sugar is melted and caramelized. Add bananas and cook slowly 1 to 2 minutes until heated and glazed. Sprinkle lightly with cinnamon. Add rum. Ignite. Spoon liquid over bananas until flames die out, about 1 minute. Serve warm over firm vanilla or coffee ice cream.

Makes 2 servings

PEARS AU CHOCOLAT

2 fresh pears
½ cup water
¼ cup sugar
½ teaspoon vanilla extract
 Nut Filling (optional, recipe follows)
 Creamy Chocolate Sauce (recipe follows)
 Whipped topping (optional)

Core pears from bottom, but leave stems intact; peel. Slice small amount from bottom of each pear to make a flat base. In small saucepan large enough for pears to stand upright, stir together water and sugar; add pears. Cover; cook over low heat 15 to 20 minutes or until pears are tender (cooking time will depend on size and ripeness of pears). Remove from heat; add vanilla. Cool pears in syrup. Refrigerate. To serve, drain pears. Spoon Nut Filling into pears, if desired. Place in serving dish; spoon Creamy Chocolate Sauce over top. Garnish with whipped topping, if desired.

Makes 2 servings

Nut Filling: In small bowl, stir together 3 tablespoons finely chopped nuts, 1 tablespoon powdered sugar and ½ teaspoon milk until mixture is well blended.

Creamy Chocolate Sauce: In small saucepan, combine 3 tablespoons sugar, 3 tablespoons water and 2 tablespoons butter or margarine. Cook over low heat, stirring constantly, until mixture comes to full boil. Remove from heat; stir in ⅔ cup **HERSHEY'S® MINI CHIPS® Semi-Sweet Chocolate.** Stir until chocolate is completely melted.

Makes about ½ cup

LOVERS' CARAMEL DESSERT

1½ cups shredded Gjetost cheese
1 cup heavy cream
1 sheet frozen puff pastry
2 large baking apples, cored
    and sliced
2 tablespoons melted butter or
    margarine
2 tablespoons light brown sugar
1 tablespoon light corn syrup
1 tablespoon lemon juice
½ teaspoon ground cinnamon
1 tablespoon granulated sugar
½ teaspoon vanilla extract

In small saucepan, combine 1 cup cheese with heavy cream. Heat, stirring, until cheese is melted. (*Do not let mixture boil.*) Pour into bowl. Cover immediately with plastic wrap. Refrigerate several hours or overnight.

Thaw pastry according to package directions. Meanwhile, combine apples, melted butter, brown sugar, corn syrup, lemon juice and cinnamon. Toss lightly to coat apples.

Press pastry into bottom of 9-inch heart-shaped baking pan, making pastry come up sides to create a 1-inch rim. Spoon apples into center of pastry. If desired, arrange in overlapping rows.

Bake at 400°F for 20 minutes, until apples are tender and pastry is golden. Remove from oven and sprinkle with remaining ½ cup Gjetost cheese. Cool on wire rack for 10 minutes. Remove tart from pan; cool for a few minutes longer on wire rack. Serve warm or at room temperature.

Just before serving, combine Gjetost cream mixture with 1 tablespoon granulated sugar and vanilla. Beat until soft peaks form. Serve with tart.

Makes 2 servings, with leftovers

Favorite recipe from **Norseland Foods, Inc.**

MANDARIN ORANGE ALMOND SHORTCAKE

1 can (11 ounces) DOLE®
    Mandarin Orange Segments,
    undrained
1 DOLE® Orange
2 tablespoons orange-flavored
    liqueur
1 tablespoon brown sugar
2 teaspoons cornstarch
    Dash of ground nutmeg
2 slices pound cake
2 scoops vanilla ice cream

• Drain syrup from mandarin oranges into small saucepan.

• Grate peel and juice orange. Measure ¼ teaspoon orange peel and ⅓ cup juice; add to saucepan with liqueur, sugar, cornstarch and nutmeg. Stir to blend. Cook, stirring, until sauce boils and thickens. Cool slightly. Add mandarin oranges.

• Place a slice of pound cake on each of two dessert plates. Mound with a scoop of ice cream. Top with orange sauce.

Makes 2 servings

Prep time: 10 minutes
Cook time: 5 minutes

Acknowledgments

*The publishers would like to thank the companies
and organizations listed below for the use of their recipes
in this publication.*

American Dairy Association
American Egg Board
American Lamb Council
Armour Swift-Eckrich
Borden Kitchens, Borden, Inc.
California Apricot Advisory Board
Canned Food Information Council
Clear Springs Trout Company
The Dannon Company, Inc.
Del Monte Corporation
Dole Food Company, Inc.
Filippo Berio Olive Oil
Hershey Chocolate U.S.A.
Kahlúa Liqueur
Kraft General Foods, Inc.
Lawry's® Foods, Inc.
Thomas J. Lipton Co.
Magic Seasoning Blends™
McIlhenny Company

Nabisco Foods Group
National Fisheries Institute
National Live Stock and Meat
   Board
National Pork Producers Council
National Turkey Federation
Norseland Foods, Inc.
Northwest Cherry Growers
Oklahoma Peanut Commission
Oscar Mayer Foods Corporation
The Procter & Gamble
   Company, Inc.
StarKist Seafood Company
The Sugar Association, Inc.
Sunkist Growers, Inc.
USA Rice Council
Western New York Apple Growers
   Association, Inc.

Photo Credits

*The publishers would like to thank the companies and
organizations listed below for the use of their photographs
in this publication.*

American Egg Board
American Lamb Council
Borden Kitchens, Borden, Inc.
Clear Springs Trout Company
Dole Food Company, Inc.
Kahlúa Liqueur
Kraft General Foods, Inc.
Thomas J. Lipton Co.
National Fisheries Institute

National Live Stock and Meat
   Board
National Pork Producers Council
National Turkey Federation
Northwest Cherry Growers
Oscar Mayer Foods Corporation
The Procter & Gamble
   Company, Inc.
Sunkist Growers, Inc.

INDEX

America's Cut with Balsamic Vinegar, 35
Apricot and Pork Salad, 22
Apricot Smoothie, 90

Bagel Pizza, 25
Bagel Toppers, 12
Basic Beef Mixture, 78
Basic Crêpes, 72
Beef
  Basic Beef Mixture, 78
  Beef Kabobs over Lemon Rice, 30
  Beef Ragout, 77
  Beef Stroganoff, 79
  Beef, Tomato and Basil Salad, 27
  Easy Beef and Broccoli Stir-Fry, 76
  Easy Beef Stroganoff, 33
  Flank Steak Teriyaki with Savory
    Rice, 32
  Herb-Seasoned Steak with Savory
    Squash, 73
  Japanese Beef Salad, 19
  Mardi Gras Beef Broil, 36
  Oriental Pepper Steak, 42
  Peppered Beef, 79
  Quick Beef Sauté, 76
  Rolled Veal Surprise, 42
  Round Steak for Four Different
    Meals, 76
  Saucy Steak and Pasta, 75
  Shape-Up Steak with Stir-Fried
    Spinach, 41
  Single-Pan Spaghetti, 35
  Strapping Soup, 30
  Tangy Eye Round Steak, 78
  Veal Piccata, 38
Beverages
  Apricot Smoothie, 90
  Breakfast Nog, 9
  Hawaiian Sunrise, 90
  Peanut Butter-Banana Shake, 9
  Strawberry-Banana Shake, 85
  24-Hour Juice Sensation, 84
Black Bean Sauced Seafood, 63
Bran Muffins, 75
Breads
  Bran Muffins, 75
  Chocolate Chunk Banana Bread, 15
Breakfast Nog, 9
Breakfast Parfait, 9
Broiled Cheese 'n Turkey Sandwich, 26
Buttermilk Pepper Dressing, 24

Cancun Chicken, 56
Cheese-Bacon Soufflé, 6
Cheese-Turkey Crêpes, 70
Cheesy Vegetable Crêpes, 72
Chef's Salad, 22
Chicken (see also **Turkey**)
  Cancun Chicken, 56
  Chicken and Vegetable Stew, 47

Chicken Paprika, 47
Chicken Rosemary, 51
Chicken "Satay" Salad, 26
Chicken Scaparella, 44
Cool 'n' Crunchy Luncheon Salad,
  28
Cornish Hens with Fruity Pilaf
  Stuffing, 59
Grilled Chicken Skewers, 48
Lite-Stuffed Chicken Breasts, 53
Quesadilla Grande, 54
Quick Sweet and Sour Chicken, 48
Sesame Chicken in Pitas, 29
Soft Taco Sandwiches, 19
Turkey-Cranberry Club Sandwiches,
  16
Zesty Pasta with Ricotta, 58
Chocolate
  Chocolate Chip-Peanut Butter
    Sauce, 86
  Chocolate Chunk Banana Bread, 15
  Chocolate Coeur à la Crème with
    Strawberry Sauce, 89
  Chocolate-Cream Bagel Spread, 12
  Chocolate Lover's Mousse for Two,
    89
  Chocolate-Peanut Butter Sauce, 86
  Creamy Chocolate Sauce, 91
  Jumbo Chunky Cookies, 86
  KAHLÚA® Tiramisu for Two, 84
  KAHLÚA® White Chocolate
    Fondue, 90
  Mocha-Peanut Butter Sauce, 86
  ONE BOWL® Brownies, 87
  Pears au Chocolat, 91
  Praline Brownies, 82
Citrus, Avocado & Bacon Salad, 28
Cookies & Brownies
  Jumbo Chunky Cookies, 86
  ONE BOWL® Brownies, 87
  Praline Brownies, 82
Cool 'n' Crunchy Luncheon Salad,
  28
Cornish Hens with Fruity Pilaf
  Stuffing, 59
Crab Bagel Spread, 12
Cream of Wheat® à la Mode, 14
Creamy Chocolate Sauce, 91

Desserts (see also **Beverages; Cookies
  & Brownies**)
  Chocolate Coeur à la Crème with
    Strawberry Sauce, 89
  Chocolate Lover's Mousse for Two,
    89
  Fresh Yogurt Sundae, 90
  KAHLÚA® Tiramisu for Two,
    84
  KAHLÚA® White Chocolate
    Fondue, 90
  Lovers' Caramel Dessert, 92
  Mandarin Orange Almond
    Shortcake, 92
  Miniature Cheesecakes, 88
  Pears au Chocolat, 91
  Quick Apple Tart, 85
  Special Bananas Foster, 91

Sweet Cherries Romanoff-Style, 85
Yogurt and Apple Dessert, 85

Easy Beef and Broccoli Stir-Fry, 76
Easy Beef Stroganoff, 33
Easy, Elegant Egg Bake, 15

Fish (*see also* **Shellfish**)
   Garden Tuna Grazer, 20
   Halibut Marengo, 64
   Microwaved Salmon Steaks with
     Mushrooms, 64
   Microwaved Trout Amandine, 68
   Quick Mediterranean Fish, 63
   Rainbow Trout Parmesan, 65
   Salmon with Chive Sauce, 66
   Soft Taco Sandwiches, 19
   Swordfish Steaks with Dill-Mustard
     Sauce, 66
   Tuna au Gratin for Two, 62
   Tuna Chowder for One, 65
   Turkey-Cranberry Club Sandwiches, 16
Flank Steak Teriyaki with Savory Rice,
   32
Freeze 'n Bake Turkey Cutlets or Slices,
   80
Fresh Strawberry Banana Omelets, 4
Fresh Yogurt Sundae, 90
Fruit and Honey-Peanut Butter Sauce,
   86

Garden Shrimp Salad, 18
Garden Tuna Grazer, 20
Golden Ham Sandwich, 18
Grilled Chicken Skewers, 48

Halibut Marengo, 64
Ham
   Golden Ham Sandwich, 18
   Ham and Cheese Quesadillas, 14
   Ham Carrot Fettuccini, 35
   Mini Turkey Ham Quiche, 10
   The California Classic, 21
   Turkey Cordon Bleu, 80
Hawaiian Sunrise, 90
Herb-Seasoned Steak with Savory
   Squash, 73
Huevos con Salsa, 12
Hurry-Up Thuringer and Bean Soup,
   36

Individual Soufflés, 81
Italian Omelet, 7

Japanese Beef Salad, 19
Jumbo Chunky Cookies, 86

KAHLÚA®Tiramisu for Two, 84
KAHLÚA® White Chocolate Fondue,
   90

Lite-Stuffed Chicken Breasts, 53
Louie Dressing, 25
Lovers' Caramel Dessert, 92

Make-Ahead French Toast, 11
Mandarin Orange Almond Shortcake, 92

Mardi Gras Beef Broil, 36
Mexican Egg Muffin, 6
Microwaved Salmon Steaks with
   Mushrooms, 64
Microwaved Trout Amandine, 68
Miniature Cheesecakes, 88
Mini-Loaves Olé, 79
Mini Turkey Ham Quiche, 10
Mocha-Peanut Butter Sauce, 86

Nut Filling, 91

ONE BOWL® Brownies, 87
1 Potato . . . , 57
Orange-Cream Bagel Spread, 12
Oriental Pepper Steak, 42

Pasta
   Chicken and Vegetable Stew, 47
   Easy Beef Stroganoff, 33
   Garden Shrimp Salad, 18
   Ham Carrot Fettuccini, 35
   Saucy Steak and Pasta, 75
   Single-Pan Spaghetti, 35
   Vegetable Medley Pasta, 38
   Zesty Pasta with Ricotta, 58
Peanut Butter and Jelly Sauce, 86
Peanut Butter-Banana Shake, 9
Peanut Butter Sauce, 86
Peanut Butter Topper, 12
Pears au Chocolat, 91
Peppered Beef, 79
Pita in the Morning, 14
Pizza Eggs, 9
Pork (*see also* **Ham; Sausage**)
   America's Cut with Balsamic
     Vinegar, 35
   Apricot and Pork Salad, 22
   Pork Medallions with Dijon-Dill
     Sauce, 33
   Pork Smittane, 43
   Pork Tenderloin with Gingersnap
     Gravy, 40
   Tasty Pork Ragout, 41
Praline Brownies, 82

Quesadilla Grande, 54
Quick Apple Tart, 85
Quick Beef Sauté, 76
Quick Mediterranean Fish, 63
Quick Sweet and Sour Chicken, 48

Rainbow Trout Parmesan, 65
Rice
   Beef Kabobs over Lemon Rice, 30
   Black Bean Sauced Seafood, 63
   Chicken Paprika, 47
   Cornish Hens with Fruity Pilaf
     Stuffing, 59
   Festival Shrimp and Saffron Rice,
     60
   Flank Steak Teriyaki with Savory
     Rice, 32
   Peppered Beef, 79
   Quick Sweet and Sour Chicken,
     48
   Tasty Pork Ragout, 41

Rice *continued*
  Thai for Two, 54
  Turkey Waldorf Salad, 24
  Turkey with Wild Rice, 74
Rolled Veal Surprise, 42
Round Steak for Four Different Meals, 76

Salads
  Apricot and Pork Salad, 22
  Beef, Tomato and Basil Salad, 27
  Chef's Salad, 22
  Chicken "Satay" Salad, 26
  Citrus, Avocado & Bacon Salad, 28
  Cool 'n' Crunchy Luncheon Salad, 28
  Garden Shrimp Salad, 18
  Japanese Beef Salad, 19
  Shrimp Louie, 25
  South-of-the-Border Shrimp Salad, 20
  Turkey Waldorf Salad, 24
  Vegetable Cottage Cheese Salad, 20
Salmon with Chive Sauce, 66
Sandwiches
  Bagel Pizza, 25
  Broiled Cheese 'n Turkey Sandwich, 26
  Garden Tuna Grazer, 20
  Golden Ham Sandwich, 18
  Mexican Egg Muffin, 6
  Pita in the Morning, 14
  Sesame Chicken in Pitas, 29
  Soft Taco Sandwiches, 19
  The California Classic, 21
  Turkey-Cranberry Club Sandwiches, 16
  Turkey Tomato Melts, 29
Satay Dressing, 26
Saucy Steak and Pasta, 75
Sausage
  Hurry-Up Thuringer and Bean Soup, 36
  Italian Omelet, 7
  Sausage Brunch Crêpes, 10
  The California Classic, 21
  Vegetable Medley Pasta, 38
Sausage Brunch Crêpes, 10
Savory Egg Puffs, 10
Seductive Shrimp & Crab, 69
Sesame Chicken in Pitas, 29
Shape-Up Steak with Stir-Fried Spinach, 41
Shellfish
  Black Bean Sauced Seafood, 63
  Crab Bagel Spread, 12
  Festival Shrimp and Saffron Rice, 60
  Garden Shrimp Salad, 18
  Seductive Shrimp & Crab, 69
  Shrimp Diane, 69
  Shrimp Louie, 25
  Soft Taco Sandwiches, 19
  South-of-the-Border Shrimp Salad, 20
Shrimp Diane, 69
Shrimp Louie, 25
Single-Pan Spaghetti, 35
Soft Taco Sandwiches, 19

Soups
  Chicken and Vegetable Stew, 47
  Hurry-Up Thuringer and Bean Soup, 36
  Strapping Soup, 30
  Tuna Chowder for One, 65
South-of-the-Border Shrimp Salad, 20
Southwestern Lamb Grill, 37
Special Bananas Foster, 91
Spicy Orange Sauce, 81
Strapping Soup, 30
Strawberry-Banana Shake, 85
Strawberry Sauce, 89
Sweet Cherries Romanoff-Style, 85
Swiss Irish Pancakes, 78
Swordfish Steaks with Dill-Mustard Sauce, 66

Take-Along Breakfast Special, 7
Tangy Eye Round Steak, 78
Tasty Pork Ragout, 41
Tex-Mex Turkey Casserole, 53
Thai for Two, 54
The California Classic, 21
Toasted Almond Sauce, 81
Tuna au Gratin for Two, 62
Tuna Chowder for One, 65
Turkey (*see also* **Chicken**)
  Broiled Cheese 'n Turkey Sandwich, 26
  Cheese-Turkey Crêpes, 70
  Chef's Salad, 22
  Cool 'n' Crunchy Luncheon Salad, 28
  Freeze 'n Bake Turkey Cutlets or Slices, 80
  Mini-Loaves Olé, 79
  Mini Turkey Ham Quiche, 10
  1 Potato . . . , 57
  Tex-Mex Turkey Casserole, 53
  Thai for Two, 54
  The California Classic, 21
  Turkey à l'Orange, 57
  Turkey and Fruit Skillet Delight, 58
  Turkey and Veggies in Creamy Dill Sauce, 56
  Turkey Cashew Cutlets, 59
  Turkey Cordon Bleu, 80
  Turkey-Cranberry Club Sandwiches, 16
  Turkey Medallions with Cumberland Sauce, 50
  Turkey Normande, 46
  Turkey-Olive Ragout en Crust, 52
  Turkey Parmesan, 44
  Turkey Parmigiana In-a-Hurry, 81
  Turkey Tomato Melts, 29
  Turkey Waldorf Salad, 24
  Turkey with Wild Rice, 74
24-Hour Juice Sensation, 84

Vegetable Cottage Cheese Salad, 20
Vegetable Medley Pasta, 38

Yogurt and Apple Dessert, 85

Zesty Pasta with Ricotta, 58